"This is *Chicken Soup for the* [illegible] with *Cruise Selling for Dummies.* Novice or expert, young or old, this is a must read. Learn the real "how to be a cruise ship selling pro" from the real expert with more than twenty-five years of selling with a heart. Lori guides you through every step of understanding and meeting your clients' needs. Follow her steps and you too will become a cruise pro."

– Jan Tuck
Manager, Princess Cruises

"Lori is one of the most knowledgeable cruise gurus I know and this book is the culmination of her years of experience. I highly recommend this practical guide to anyone new to the industry who wants to learn to sell cruises from the best."

– Andi McClure-Mysza
President, MTravel.com,
the host division of Montrose Travel

"I have known Lori Pelentay as a personal friend and cruise colleague for some twenty-five years. Going back to our days working together at Princess Cruises in the 1980s, we gained a mutual respect for each other's thoroughness and expertise. Lori has carried those qualities into her own cruise agency while acquiring a vast amount of first-hand cruising experience. Her wide range of procedural and practical knowledge is shared in this handbook."

– Kim Johnson
President, Cruise Navigators

HOW TO SELL CRUISES

step by step

SECOND EDITION

Lori Berberian Pelentay

How To Sell Cruises Step-by-Step
A Beginner's Guide to Becoming a
"Cruise-Selling" Travel Agent
Second Edition

All rights reserved, including the right of reproduction, in whole or in part in any form, without written permission of the publisher, except in the case of brief quotations embedded in critical articles and reviews. Requests to the Author for permission should be addressed to Lori Berberian Pelentay, P.O. Box 1434, Sierra Madre, CA 91024, or online at lori@berberian.com.

Limit of Liability/Disclaimer of Warranty: While the Author has used her best efforts in preparing this book, she makes no representations or warranties with respect to the accuracy or completeness of the contents of this book and specifically disclaims any implied warranties of merchantability, or fitness for a particular purpose. No warranty may be created or extended by sales representatives or written sales materials. The advice and strategies contained herein may not be suitable for your situation. You should consult with a professional where appropriate. Neither the Publisher nor Author shall be liable for any loss of profit or any other commercial damages, including but not limited to special, incidental, consequential or other damages.

Copyright © 2020 Lori Berberian Pelentay
ISBN: 978-1-946462-13-8 (trade paperback)

Published by Soul's Road Press
www.soulsroadpress.com

Contents

This book is dedicated to Jan Tuck,
my first teacher and great friend.

Also to my parents, Russ and Frances Berberian,
who gave me my love of cruising.

Introduction

I AM SITTING ON MY BALCONY aboard the *Sapphire Princess* as I type this. The wake of the ship spreads out behind us like a jewel-encrusted bridal train, and I can feel the spray of the Pacific Ocean on my face. Ah, this is the life! After dozens of cruises, my heart still quickens every time I see the smokestack of a ship and catch my first glimpse of her sitting at the pier, waiting for the passengers to board.

I've been in the cruise industry for more than twenty-eight years, first working for Princess Cruises in the corporate offices, and then working on board the *Pacific Princess* for a year in the Mediterranean. After my time at Princess, friends and family would still call me for information on cruises, so I eventually started selling them as a travel agent, and after my divorce, opened my own agency, Kensington Cruises. I joined host agency, Montrose Travel, in 2006 and had the opportunity to meet many new travel agents eager to learn about the business and travel. Once these new agents heard about my experience, they would inundate my in-box with questions about cruising, cruise lines, selling cruises, and every other kind of question you could imagine. Finally, one of these agents, Julia Pfeiffer, encouraged me to write this book so I could put all of this knowledge to good use and help those just beginning in the business.

If you are reading this, chances are you are beginning your adventure in the travel industry. Whether you are jumping in with both feet and making this your full time career, or just doing this as a part-time diversion, I hope the information contained in this book will start you off in the right direction selling cruises. In these pages I will offer practical tips on how to organize your office and paperwork, how to read deck plans, information on the different cruise lines, and how to make the most money for your time.

So, if you are ready, let's get started selling cruises!

Why Cruises?

THE TRAVEL INDUSTRY HAS taken several huge blows in the last twenty years. In the "old days," travel agents used to make the bulk of their money selling air tickets and putting together tours. In 1978, the airlines decided to stop paying commissions to travel agents, and decimated the income potential for most brick-and-mortar agencies. (A *brick-and-mortar agency* is another name for a travel agency that has a store front in a commercial location, as opposed to a home-based agency.)

Over the years, I have dabbled in selling all kinds of travel, including tours, airline tickets, hotels, and cruises. My experience is that, as a travel agent, I *personally* make more money for my time selling cruises. That's not to say that the travel agent down the street is making a wonderful living selling corporate travel, or the local travel agency downtown is doing very well, thank you very much, selling any kind of travel their clients are looking for – for me, personally, however, cruises have been the most profitable. Why? I have become an expert in my field. I specialize in this form of travel, so that when it comes time to match my client with a cruise, I don't have to spend valuable research time trying to figure it out for them; I instinctively know how best to fit them to their ideal cruise vacation.

I can't tell you how many times I have spent hours and hours researching various elements of a trip to Europe, including air, train, hotels, sightseeing, etc., when for less than half that amount of time, I could have booked them on a beautiful cruise and received twice the commission! Plus, with a cruise, I know they are going to get a wonderful experience *if I've matched them well with the right cruise line and itinerary.*

The cruise lines want their passengers to use travel agents. Yes, the cruise lines have opened up telephone lines for passengers to book directly with them, but most of them will allow a travel agent to take over the booking if the passenger gives the travel agent permission to do so. Why? There is a lot of peripheral work that the travel agent does to make sure the passenger's cruise vacation goes smoothly, and the cruise lines know this. They don't want to deal with all the little questions your clients are going to have prior to their cruise; that's why they pay you, the travel agent, a commission, so you can handle that for them. In the late 1990s, Renaissance Cruise Lines tried to bypass the travel agents and encouraged passengers to book directly with the cruise line. They very soon learned the error of their ways (Renaissance folded soon after the September 11th events), and when Frank del Rio and Joe Watters started Oceania Cruise Lines, they made it a point to apologize to the travel agent community and woo travel agents back.

You are the lifeline between potential passengers and the various cruise lines out there. They want your business, so they have put into place wonderful training courses for you to learn how to sell their products. We will discuss these later in the book. I encourage you to take advantage of these online training opportunities as well as CLIA's (Cruise Line International Association) trainings; they are an invaluable way to learn the business of selling cruises, and will complement what you will learn here.

More on that later….

First Things First

Okay, you want to sell cruises. Here's the first thing you *have* to do...

Go on a cruise. Yes, get thyself on a ship any way you can. I have been saying this for twenty-five years...if you really want to understand how to sell cruises, you have to experience one so you can talk about it! I am sitting on the *Sapphire Princess* right now, but can you believe I paid the full price for it? Not a travel agent rate! That's because if you time it right, sometimes the passenger fare is better than a travel agent rate...hard to believe, but true. The best rates can be found in January and February for Mexico and the Caribbean, then May or September for Alaska (and sometimes Europe). Cruise fares go down again in Europe, Mexico, and Caribbean in early November (before Thanksgiving) and again in December (during the first three weeks before Christmas week). For the times in between, check out the weekly e-mails the cruise lines send out for the last-minute specials. I have seen Europe cruises for $499 for twelve-night sailings if you can go last minute!

There's nothing like experiencing every aspect of a cruise...from embarkation to disembarkation, there's a certain "ritual" that takes place that can only be experienced rather than described. Even if it's a three- or four-day cruise, you will at least get the experience of being on a ship – although a seven-day cruise is preferable. Can you deduct it as a business expense? You betcha! (Although I would check with your accountant just to make sure). I have cruised in every type of stateroom just so I can share about the experience. I must admit, though, that I've sailed only once in an inside stateroom; once was enough for claustrophobic me! If you can, try to sail in an ocean view stateroom or, if possible, a balcony room. Believe me, you sell what you know! You'll be able to wax poetic about having breakfast on your balcony, or hearing the sound of waves as you drift off to sleep! (Although, right now I'm watching a helicopter land on the ship to pick up a passenger in need of immediate medical attention…hmm. Not what I pictured viewing from my balcony!)

So, my advice for the best learning experience is to *cruise*!

Cruise Line and CLIA's Training Courses

THE NEXT THING YOU NEED to do is take some time and take the cruise line-sponsored training classes. The two most popular courses are POLAR online for Princess Cruises, Holland America, and Cunard, and University of WOW for Royal Caribbean (RCCL), Celebrity, and Azamara. If you are going to sell Carnival Cruise Line, you will want to learn their system as well. I personally started with Princess' POLAR online because once you complete their coursework, *you get a free cruise*! *Yes*, you read that correctly! Once you attain Commodore status, you get to choose from anywhere Princess sails, provided it is on their list of available cruises to choose from. (If you go through Cunard's training class as well, you can choose a Cunard cruise, too! Yes, that includes the *Queen Elizabeth*, or the *Queen Mary* sailing the transatlantic!!)

The very top of my bucket list was an Australia/New Zealand cruise, so sure enough, they offered a two-week cruise as one of the choices available. Mind you, this was a $2500 *per person* cruise if I had to pay for it, and it was absolutely *free*! I just had to pay gratuities and airfare, plus any other incidental expenses. It was truly the trip of a lifetime, and I couldn't have done it without the help from Princess' Commodore Program. I've even seen a thirty-day Asian Wonderland cruise offered to Commodores, *all for free*! So, start on those POLAR online courses, and work your way to a fabulous cruise for you and your loved one. It's time well spent! (I would hold off for a truly spectacular itinerary and not waste it on just a Caribbean or Mexico cruise…be imaginative!)

If you are with a host agency, they will need to give you a sign-on for POLAR and approve you through their system before you can begin. If you have your own agency, you just need to sign up for POLAR with your CLIA or IATA number, plus all applicable information. (But really, if you are a beginning agent, you really should think of joining a host agency…don't do it all by yourself).

University of WOW is also very important, as it is the booking system for Royal Caribbean, Celebrity, and Azamara. With these two training courses (POLAR and U of Wow), plus Carnival Cruise Lines, you will have most of the mainstream cruise lines under your belt.

The other mainstream cruise line I have not mentioned is Norwegian Cruise Line's (NCL) program. I will talk about preferred suppliers later on in the book, but NCL is not a cruise line I typically sell, so I have not taken their courses. You will need to decide which Mass Market cruise lines you want to represent, and those are the classes you will want to take so you are fully versed in booking them using their online booking portals.

With that having been said, I do recommend using both the online portal as well as the cruise line's phone reservation systems as you are beginning in this business. There is *so* much to know that you can't possibly assimilate it all in the very beginning, so it behooves you to have the cruise line's reservations agents look over your bookings once you make them to ensure you have all your T's crossed and I's dotted. I will say this several times throughout this book, but there are no stupid questions, only unhappy passengers if you have not done your due diligence – so *ask questions*! The reservations agents work with these ships and itineraries every day, so they know so much more than you could ever hope to learn in a short period of time; use their expertise to your benefit. Even if it takes a little more time for each booking in the beginning…it's well worth it to ensure a happy passenger.

The Cruise Line International Association (CLIA) also has training classes as part of their agent designation program. You can earn your Accredited Cruise Counselor, Master Cruise Counselor, Luxury Cruise Counselor, and other designations through them. I highly suggest taking these courses and obtaining at least the Accredited Cruise Counselor designation. It shows that you take your career seriously, and have put in time and effort to get to know the cruise industry as a whole.

The classes will teach you how to sell cruises in general, as well as the ins and outs of the industry. They also require ship inspections as part of the designation, so you get to see other ships besides those that you have cruised. You will need to sign up with CLIA first, showing your intention to attain your designation.

CLIA has conferences every year where you can go to Florida or Vancouver (or Seattle, depending on the year), and get *all* of these classes out of the way, plus the required ship inspections. What fun these conventions are, especially if you love ships! They very often have a dozen or more ships in port for you to inspect to compare and get a feeling for. These inspections are invaluable, especially if you don't have time to cruise on every single cruise line. Most days you will have lunch onboard one of these ships, so you can see what their cuisine is like, and believe me, they pull out all the stops to impress you!

Try to get to a CLIA convention as soon as you can, make sure to fly in a day or so earlier to take your CLIA designation classes there, and sign up for as many ship inspections with as many different cruise lines as possible (i.e., don't inspect two Princess ships, or two RCCL ships, but one of each, plus as many other cruise lines as they offer and time permits). I promise you, this convention will help you sell more cruises and get you so excited for what you are doing…it's well worth every single penny!

How Cruises Work

MOST PEOPLE DON'T REALIZE that ships cruise seven days a week. On "turnaround day," a ship arrives into port usually by 7 a.m. and disembarks all the previous cruises' passengers. The staff cleans like crazy to get all the staterooms and public rooms ready to go for the next cruise, and then by noon or 1 p.m., embarks all the new passengers in order to sail by 5 or 6 p.m.!

Occasionally a ship will arrive into a port and have an overnight; Venice, Italy is a common turnaround port where cruise lines will have an in-port overnight so their guests can use the ship as a hotel. While this is great for the passengers, the staff still needs to have the ship ready in a matter of hours, because there are no days in between where there are no passengers onboard. This means the room stewards, dining room staff, buffet staff, officers, and all other essential shipboard staff never receives a full day off. They typically have three, six, or nine-month contracts, and work seven days a week! They are the hardest working people I have ever met and most work *for tips only*! Can you imagine working fourteen hours a day, seven days a week, and knowing that your pay is dependent on whether or not the people you are serving like you, and are willing to give you $3 a day, per person, for all your hard work? I say, God bless them! I always make sure to let them know how much I appreciate them, and usually pre-tip my room stewards and dining room staff (if I will have the same team throughout the cruise), in addition to what is "required" by the cruise line. (More on tipping/gratuities on page 66).

Cruise Lines

One of the most common questions I get asked is, "Which cruise line should I sell?"

Good question, but a difficult one to give a generic answer to. It all depends on your clientele. I know an agent who has a predominantly younger crowd, with families and limited income; she specializes in Carnival Cruise Lines and Royal Caribbean. Another agent I know works with the local retirement community whose members have more time to travel–but again, limited income. She leans towards Holland America and the longer voyages of Princess Cruises. Yet another agent draws most of his clientele from Laguna Beach and Newport Beach, where their net income is in the six figures. He leans towards Crystal Cruises and the smaller ships of Regent Seven Seas, Seabourn, or Oceania.

These travel agents have made choices to have preferred suppliers that they predominantly use for their type of clients; however, these cruise lines are not the only ones that fit their type of clientele. The benefit of having preferred suppliers is that the more you sell per year of a particular cruise line, the higher commission you get. This is done on a year-by-year basis, so even the biggest agencies need to prove themselves every year to earn the higher commission. (More on preferred suppliers later.)

There are three different categories of cruise lines in the market today: Mass Market, Premium, and Luxury. I have included brief descriptions on some of the cruise lines below to help you discern which one might work best for your particular clients. I cannot stress enough the benefit of you spending some time on each individual cruise line's website; they have spent huge amounts of money with advertising agencies developing their websites to give you the features and benefits of their ships and programs onboard. Perhaps choose one or two cruise lines a day and read what each has to say about their ships, onboard activities, and the type of clients that prefer their products. It's also good to know which cruise lines go where; for example, the small Luxury cruise lines might only have two or three ships, and spend their time in the Caribbean and Mediterranean only. The large cruise lines with over a dozen ships are able to place them all over the world. It will be time well spent for you.

Following is my personal opinion and summary of the major cruise lines.

I have included target markets to help give you quick tips on who works best with each cruise line. Most cruise lines have pools, but I have indicated those that have special water attractions such as slides, water parks, etc. Most also have spas, but if their spa is particularly good, I have indicated that as well. I have also mentioned those that have Broadway-style revue shows under *Entertainment*. If the cruise line has a particularly great past-passenger program, I have indicated that as well, as most cruise lines have one; some have better benefits than others, so it's worth noting (and joining!) Please refer to the individual websites for these programs; it's important to be aware of them, especially if you are booking a cruise for a well-traveled passenger who is a member of one. The benefits at the top tiers can be extensive (such as free laundry, priority embarkation and disembarkation, onboard credits, and special parties, among others), and are important to consider as part of the offerings when discussing an appropriate cruise for your passengers.

As far as price range, I have followed the following guidelines (of course, you may find a spectacular sale, but this is the typical range of cruise fare for 7 days, per person); Europe and other exotic itineraries may be higher:

- Budget: $0-$500 for 7 days
- Mid-range: $500-$3000
- Luxury: $3000-higher

MASS MARKET

Princess Cruises

www.princess.com

all age groups, retired, singles, married, honeymooners, family reunions, entertainment, past-passenger program, port-intensive (in some cases), spa, chef's table, foodies (alternative dining), adults only area (for a fee), past passenger program, children's program, mid-range

One of the pioneers in cruising, Princess started in the 1970s and revolutionized the idea of cruising with their participation in the iconic *Love Boat* television series. The first few episodes (as well as several "location" episodes) were filmed onboard their *Pacific Princess* and *Island Princess*, and the TV series used the model of *Pacific Princess* as their template. I remember, early in my Princess Cruises days, having our holiday party on the set of *The Love Boat* and credit the show with fueling the fire in my desire to work in the cruise industry!

Princess is one of the top two cruise lines (along with Royal Caribbean) that I consider having something for everyone. I have very wealthy clients who will only cruise Princess, as well as large families who love the value for price. They currently have eighteen ships, and have ship capacities ranging from 700 to 3,600 passengers. Why is this important? My luxury clients appreciate the small ships of Princess because the level of service is comparable to the more expensive, Luxury cruise lines, but for half the price.

Princess is a fantastic cruise line for families; this is actually one of the things they specialize in, and I've put many family reunions on Princess simply because of the variety of options for every age. A quick glimpse at the *Princess Patter*, their daily newspaper, shows the variety of activities to choose from. Pilates to trivia, napkin folding to bridge, scavenger hunts to ice carving, the list goes on and on! I have chosen Princess as my cruise line of choice to teach you how to read deck plans, simply because this is one cruise line that will serve you well for most clients. You tend to sell what you learn with, so it will be a good go-to cruise line for you in the beginning of your career. (Please don't forget, however, to always ask your client if they have ever cruised before, and if so, what cruise line. Some people prefer other similar cruise lines, so you always want to find that out first before you start quoting prices.)

Princess has now introduced Medallion Class on some of their ships. This is an innovative technology created to give the passengers a more streamlined way to experience their cruise. It is definitely worth your while to go online to learn about Princess' Medallion Class technology. Basically, passengers become Ocean Ready prior to their cruise by downloading the Medallion Class App from their app store on their smart phones or tablets, and once they fill out the pertinent information, they will receive an actual Medallion, either in the mail prior to the cruise, or at the pier. This will allow them to do everything from opening their stateroom doors, to finding friends and family onboard. It also offers the opportunity to order food and drinks from anywhere on the ship to be delivered right to them, and has the daily program of events right at their fingertips. There are a number of other options available with the Medallion, so if your clients are booked on a Medallion Class sailing, it behooves you to learn about this new shipboard technology.

Carnival Cruise Line

www.Carnival.com

families, all age groups, single,
married, honeymooners,
family reunions, water attractions,
entertainment, past-passenger
program, children's program,
budget to mid-range

Home of the "Fun Ships," Carnival is a huge cruise line with twenty-five ships, with capacities ranging from 2,052 passengers on the *Carnival Paradise* to 3,934 passengers on the *Carnival Vista and Carnival Horizon*. Carnival's theme is all about having fun, and they try to help you achieve that from the moment you walk on their ships! You are typically greeted by a member of the bar staff offering you the opportunity to purchase the "drink of the day," or anything that will help you achieve that state of *fun*, and they don't stop offering until the minute you disembark!

Carnival also caters to families, and offers a myriad of programs and activities that reflect this, including their fabulous water slides on each ship.

Pricing can be similar to Princess and the other family-friendly cruise lines, but you can sometimes get some great deals closer to sailing, especially for three- and four-berth staterooms, so if your clients fall into this demographic, make sure to check their prices.

Please note that student groups and groups where majority of the passengers are under the age of twenty-one are *not* a good match for Carnival Cruise Lines. Carnival has a very strict policy on needing an adult older than the age of twenty-five in each cabin when there are passengers younger than twenty-one years old traveling. There is no simple way around this policy, and they are very particular when it comes to these groups. If you are even thinking of putting one on Carnival, make sure you speak with them regarding their policies about this. If you have minors traveling, their parents or guardians must be in the same stateroom or in adjacent cabins, or you run the risk of being disembarked. *Yes*, Carnival will disembark any group that does not adhere to their very strict policy on this…believe me, I know of what I speak!

I typically put honeymooners and young people (twenty-five years and older) who want to have a good time, enjoy socializing and imbibing, and are not offended by the party atmosphere onboard Carnival. If my clients are more conservative, I will consider putting them on Princess or Royal Caribbean instead, but if they want to *party*, then Carnival may be the perfect cruise line for them.

Again, I always *ask* first, then compare the prices between all the cruise lines for similar itineraries and dates. I once made the mistake, early in my career, of putting a couple onboard who I thought would like the brand new Carnival ship with all the bells and whistles, without asking what they looked for in entertainment and night life. Unbeknownst to me, they were very conservative, and came home extremely indignant and upset with me that I would even consider putting them in such a hedonistic atmosphere. I had neglected to ask the most rudimentary of questions, and just assumed that the newness of the ship would be all the enticement they needed to enjoy themselves. I can't stress enough the importance of that first conversation during which you determine what they are looking for. For many, Carnival is the perfect solution!

Royal Caribbean Cruise Line

www.rccl.com

all age groups, family reunions, retired, single, married, honeymooners, port intensive (some itineraries), sports, foodies (alternative dining), water attractions, zip line, rock-climbing walls, ice skating, entertainment, spa,many unique offerings on Oasis-class ships, past-passenger program, children's program, mid-range

Royal Caribbean is the other top cruise line that I consider to have something for everyone. If you ask my son, he would say this is the best cruise line for kids; there are many others who might insist otherwise, but in the eyes of a seventeen-year-old, Royal Caribbean rules! Why, you may ask? The list is long, but includes a rock-climbing wall, ice skating rink, zip line across the ship, basketball court, miniature golf course…and I've only just begun. They currently hold the title of having the largest cruise ships at sea, held by the *Oasis* Class Ships at 5,402 passengers (there are 2,115 crew members – more than most ships even hold altogether!) but there are also ships that hold about 2,048 passengers in the Vision Class (some more, some less, depending on the ship).

Royal Caribbean is consistently good across the board, and I have never had a bad cruise among the sixteen-plus I have been on. They have pushed the envelope when it comes to innovations at sea with the Oasis-class ships; some people argue that the ship as a destination defeats the purpose of going on a cruise, but others just love all the opportunities that come with these mega-ships. You really have to question your client if they would enjoy such a large vessel; kids and families typically love these ships, but you have to make sure the older participants who may have cruised before are not put off by the huge numbers of passengers and overwhelming choices of activities. My son thought his *Oasis of the Seas* cruise was the best he had ever been on, while my mother (seventy-six years old and a veteran of more that a hundred cruises) really disliked the size and impersonal feeling she got. I loved both times that I sailed on the Oasis-class ships, but I am a ship-a-holic, so I love any experience at sea, with few exceptions.

RCCL has elevated the bar when it comes to alternative dining options at sea. On Oasis-class ships, there are more than twenty-seven different dining options to choose from! Some are included in the cruise fare, but many are not. There is everything from a 24-hour pizzeria and Johnny Rocket's ($), to spa cuisine for the calorie counters, to Michelin star-rated restaurants and steak houses that rival the best on land. (At a price, of course.) And if your passenger is a wine connoisseur, there are plenty of opportunities to indulge in wonderful wines by the glass or bottle. Yes, there are plenty of opportunities on board the Royal Caribbean ships to rack up the balance on those cruise cards–all while having the time of your life, of course!

Disney Cruise Line

www.disneycruise.com

families, all age groups, single, married, and honeymooners who love Disney, family reunions, exceptional children's program through age 18, foodies, water attractions, spa, adults-only areas, entertainment, mid-range to luxury

Wow. Disney Cruise Line inspires the *wow* in me! I've been on countless cruises, and this cruise was perhaps one my favorites… and this was with a sixteen-year-old boy! My twin nieces absolutely loved running around in their Disney Princess dresses the whole time, indulging at the kid's club and having their hair and makeup done at the *Bibidi-Bobidi-Boo* Salon!

Disney Cruise Line is the Ritz Carlton of cruises for families; I feel every part of this cruise is first class: from the service to the food, from the accommodations to entertainment, Disney excels.

The service is impeccable, especially considering most of the passengers were children. You need to be a special type of person to work on a Disney Cruise ship; i.e. love kids, love serving, and have a happy disposition at all times. From the room steward to the guest relations desk, everyone went over and above to make sure the cruise was magical.

The food was beyond anything I could have expected on a cruise ship that focuses on children. They of course had a children's menu, complete with hamburgers, hot dogs, pizza, pasta, and mac-and-cheese; the surprising thing was what they did for the adults. I guess they figured that they had the kids covered, so they could really go all-out for the adults. This was one of the most sophisticated menus I have seen on a family cruise ship. You never felt that you were one of thousands of meals served each day; every meal always felt like it was prepared especially for you. They had inventive sauces and food preparation, and the best of cuts of meat and fresh fish. The sides were creative and delicious, and the deserts were Disney worthy!

Entertainment was the best I've ever seen at sea, bar none. Granted, I love Disney, so the fact they were all Disney/children oriented was fine with me, but these were truly Broadway-caliber shows, entertainers, music, sets, lights, and costumes. You can only see these shows on the ships, so you really need to experience a Disney cruise to appreciate just how exceptional the entertainment is. Disney brought in magicians, comics, and other cabaret-style entertainers throughout the cruise, so there was always a fresh choice of entertainment late at night for the adults.

Speaking of adults, Disney has the best separation of "children from adult" areas of any cruise line; it is incredibly important to them that their adults onboard feel they can rest and relax, so they have made a huge effort to ensure this happens. There is an adults-only pool right outside the spa (which is also an adults-only zone) with plenty of deck chairs and a bar to serve just the right poolside adult beverages for you.

If your clients want a nice quiet dinner, then make sure to put them on second seating. It begins between 8:15 to 8:30 p.m., so those families with small children can bring them down and the children get served immediately. Then, starting between 9:00 to 9:15 p.m., the children's staff comes to take them to their individual play rooms (all age appropriate) so mom and dad (and all the other adults) can enjoy the rest of their dinner in peace. It works beautifully. Adults can also opt to have dinner in Palo's or Remi's, their alternative dining rooms serving exquisite Italian cuisine, at a cost. No one, and I mean *no one* younger than eighteen is allowed, even if their eighteenth birthday is next week!

Did I mention the Disney Princesses? Yes, they are on board, and make appearances at strategic times during the sailing. They are available for photos and autographs for adults as well as children. The line was literally around the perimeter of the ship, but everyone who waited got their turn, and even the grown-ups walked around with silly smiles on their faces for the rest of the day. Disney characters also make an appearance.

An important note on Disney is that there are no casinos on their ships; this is very important if you have clients who love to gamble when they go on vacation, so make sure to ask if this is a consideration for them.

The accommodation is the most family-friendly of any cruise line, and I wish other cruise lines would take note of it. Most of the staterooms have two separate bathrooms; one with a toilet and sink, and the other with sink and bath/shower. This is *so* helpful if someone is taking a shower and a little person has to go potty! Or a big person...you get my drift. They have multiple bedding configurations, and some staterooms are large enough to hold six people utilizing Murphy beds, upper berths, sofa beds, and the like. It is *very* important that you double-check the bedding to make sure every person has an appropriate bed; i.e. you don't want a two-year-old in an upper berth (they might fall). Same goes with a large fifteen-year-old child who will have difficulty fitting in the upper berth. Make sure to discuss the bedding options with your client when you reserve the stateroom; sometimes going up a category, or booking two lower-category rooms that are adjoining, will be a more appropriate choice for them. (We will discuss bedding configuration on page 89.) Disney also has many adjoining staterooms (with a door between the two similar to hotel rooms), which are great for families that want privacy for the adults, but still want to be able to monitor the children through the open door.

Norwegian Cruise Line

www.ncl.com

all age groups, families, retired, single, married, honeymooners, family reunions, entertainment, bowling, children's program, past-passenger program, budget to mid-range

Norwegian Cruise Line is one of the two cruise lines (besides Carnival) that have been around since the beginning of Mass Market cruising. This is the "little engine that could"! Every time I think this cruise line is going to go under, they find new sources of funding and shoot more money back into their ships and onboard programming.

If you are cruising with a large family and have some money to spend, their Haven Suites are beyond incredible! With up to 5,750 square feet, this three-bedroom "villa" includes a hot tub, living room, private deck area, three bedrooms, three and a half bathrooms, concierge, butler...the list goes on! You can add several more bedrooms depending on how many are in your party–perfect for a family reunion! For those of us who have a more "normal" budget, NCL has several unique stateroom choices, including their single staterooms on the *Norweigan Epic*; these staterooms are tiny in size, but have everything a single person needs, including a toilet, shower, and double bed. There is a shared living room area with the other single staterooms, so this is perfect for the person who doesn't spend any time in their stateroom except to sleep and change their clothes, and is out and about enjoying all the ship has to offer.

NCL was the first to come up with what they call Freestyle Dining, (also called Personal Choice Dining on Princess, or My Time Dining on RCCL) and they offer several different complementary restaurants onboard to choose from. None of their ships offer set dining times, so make sure your clients who have sailed with other cruise lines know that they will be on Freestyle Dining.

NCL was also the first cruise line to bring Broadway shows in their entirety to sea. The first show they did was *Grease*, and it was a huge hit. They now employ Broadway choreographers, and have licensing agreements with The Second City comedy troupe, Nickelodeon, and the Blue Man Group, so their entertainment is top notch.

NCL is the only cruise line that has a U.S. flagged ship. What that means to you is that this is the only cruise line that can legally cruise Hawaii in seven days. In 1886, the U.S. Government passed a law stating that no foreign flagged ship can transport passengers from one U.S. port to another (including the same port as departure) without first visiting a foreign port somewhere during that voyage. (The only exception is if the ship begins and ends their voyage in the same port without any stops; i.e. a Cruise to Nowhere). Some sources call this the Jones' Act, (which is incorrectly referenced, by the way), and others call it the Cabatoge Law, but basically it was enacted to protect U.S. flagged ships. The only problem is that now there is only one U.S. flagged ship, and that is the *Pride of America*, owned by NCL! Essentially, NCL has the only ship that is allowed to cruise the Hawaiian Islands without having to stop in a foreign port.

There have been a few concessions, however, that NCL had to make in order to get an American flagged vessel: They had to give up their casino per the request of the Hawaiian Islands and, more importantly, they have to have American employees, subject to American work laws and American taxation rates. This is incredibly expensive for them, as our work laws and minimum wages are considerably higher than other cruise lines. (All the other cruise lines, plus the other ships of NCL, can get away with not paying their room stewards and dining stewards any sort of salary, and requiring them to live exclusively off the tips the passengers pay them. That is why most of the cruise lines have taken to automatically charging tips to passenger's room accounts; the only way to avoid paying these tips is to go to the purser's office and specifically request that they be removed from your account.)

Have you noticed the work ethic of the typical American employee? They don't like to work very hard; a room steward and dining steward on a ship typically work about fourteen hours a day, seven days a week, six months at a time. When NCL brought their first batch of American employees onto the ships, there was a (for lack of a better word) revolt by the crew, and several crew members walked off at the next port of call! Needless to say, they are now training their employees extensively prior to embarking the ships, but it is still very difficult to find hard-working American personnel for the ship, and the passenger comment cards have reflected this.

NCL has worked very hard over the years to improve their Hawaiian product, and the past few clients I have booked have been very happy with their cruises. However, I do lots of pre-coaching before I allow my passengers to consider going on the NCL ship cruising to Hawaii; they know in advance that the service is not going to be similar to what they are used to on other cruise ships, and that they should just enjoy the ship as a hotel room, not as a destination. Their destination is the Hawaiian Islands that they cruise to.

Incidentally, the cruise lines have tried unsuccessfully to overturn this law for as long as I've known, and for some reason it is untouchable. I have no idea why, but it is defended as strongly as our borders are, so I do not foresee any other ships in the near future cruising this very desirable itinerary.

NCL's ships are innovative and new, there's multiple dining choices, and as of press time, they are offering several perks for cruising with them, including beverage packages, free Internet, specialty dining packages and onboard credits. They try very hard to compete in an extremely competitive marketplace. I would definitely cruise in a Villa Suite if given the chance!

Holland America Cruises
www.hollandamerica.com

retired, single, married, family reunions, past-passenger program, port-intensive (in some cases), longer cruises with days at sea, spa, culinary program with demo kitchen, children's program on select sailings during summer (Alaska) and holidays, mid-range to luxury

When I think of Holland America (HAL), I usually think of my retired or older clients. HAL wishes that weren't the case, but it is true that their demographic is decidedly older than the other Mass Market cruise lines. The feel on their ships is more quiet and soft-spoken; you won't see a myriad of pool games or activities for a younger crowd. You will see a more refined cruising experience; napkin folding rather than beach-blanket volleyball, bridge games rather than sexy-legs-by-the-pool contests!

One of their highlights is their culinary program, where the cruise line sponsors chefs to come on board and teach classes to the passengers in their demonstration kitchen. A first of its kind at sea, this has proven to be a very popular program, and HAL encourages travel agents to build groups around these chef experiences. You can even put together groups and bring your own chef onboard! What a great opportunity if you have a local restaurant or chef who might enjoy advertising this for you.

Their staterooms are a bit larger than other Mass Market cruise lines and their ships are smaller in size with fewer passengers, so you get to know people easier than on the huge mega-liners.

The staff is primarily Indonesian; they must attend a special college in Indonesia where they learn how to work at sea prior to starting on their ship. I must say that I felt they were better trained in the past. My last two HAL cruises seemed quite a bit different in their level of service, and other past passengers have remarked on this as well. This change has been noticeable since Carnival Cruise Corporation purchased HAL, so I am wondering if there might be less staffing and training done than before. In any case, having the Indonesian staff does make a difference compared to the other cruise lines that have sixty to seventy different nationalities working together.

The food is standard fare and not very imaginative, which works with the older clientele. There is an alternative restaurant, The Pinnacle Grill, where the food is exceptional, but there is an additional charge.

For most of the year there is no children's program, unless there are more than twenty children in any one age group on any given sailing. At that point, they will bring on a youth counselor. They do have an organized program during the summer months in Alaska and on the holiday sailings – again, if there are enough children. My family and I went on a Baltic cruise on the *Prinsendam* in the middle of summer. There were only two other children besides our three, so a member of the cruise staff had to entertain them for a few hours a day. They were stuck in the card room (or any room they could find that was empty). It seemed a bit haphazard, and the kids were bored, so they really had to find their entertainment ashore or with us. Don't count on a children's program during the summer in Europe unless you check with HAL first.

Celebrity Cruises
www.celebritycruises.com

Part of Royal Caribbean Corp.

all age groups, retired, single, married, honeymooners, family reunions, entertainment, past-passenger program, port-intensive, spa, foodies (alternative dining), children's program, mid-range to luxury

Celebrity Cruise Lines is owned by RCCL, but the two couldn't be more different. Celebrity is RCCL's older sister or brother and is infinitely more elegant and refined. They are trying to position themselves somewhere between Mass Market and Luxury, and their ships reflect this. The Solstice Class ships are beautiful, offering some of the best designs in stateroom and bathroom configuration I have seen. Storage abounds, especially in the bathrooms. The décor is chic, streamlined, and clean, with public areas that are a reflection of the desire to differentiate from the Mass Market feel of other cruise lines.

Celebrity's buffet area (on Solstice Class ships) is the best layout of any ship I have been on. Considering the average cruiser eats one to two meals every day at the buffet, this is an important venue. The room is large and open, and facilitates the movement of many people going through at the same time. The food is displayed beautifully, and there are several different stations where one can get freshly prepared items to order, such as eggs and omelets in the morning, or pasta and sandwiches in the afternoon and evening. Other cruise lines could take lessons from this layout!

Their alternative restaurants are imaginative and exciting. Qsine has patrons ordering off an iPad, and delivers food in test tubes, among other creative plates. There is also a delicious Italian restaurant and even a creperie! Celebrity has stated that they want to be the cruise line for foodies, and they are making substantial efforts toward this goal.

One would think Celebrity would be substantially more expensive than the other Mass Market cruise lines, but this is not the case. I have found some unbelievable deals on Celebrity, especially to the Caribbean. If you have a client who would appreciate a more refined cruising experience, make sure to check the prices on Celebrity and compare them to Princess or RCCL. (It's easy to do so on Cruising Power, Celebrity's and RCCL's reservation system for travel agents.)

If you have a family with young children, make sure to call Celebrity's reservations department to confirm whether or not there will be a children's program offered on the particular sailing you are looking at. Do not assume there will always be one, unless you are cruising during the summer months or holiday sailings.

Over the past year, all of my clients who have sailed on Celebrity have come home very happy with their cruising experience. You can sell this cruise line with confidence.

PREMIUM CRUISE LINES

Azamara and Oceania Cruise Lines

Premium lines strive to be a step above the Mass Market, but still do not reach the caliber of the Luxury cruise lines. The interesting thing about Azamara and Oceania is they have exactly the same ships (with the exception of Oceania's *Marina* and *Riviera*). When Renaissance Cruise Lines went out of business between 2001 and 2002, they had several lovely ships in their fleet, so these were snapped up by Royal Caribbean (for their new cruise line, Azamara), Princess Cruises (considered the "small ships" of Princess) and Oceania Cruise Lines. Oceania was started by the former CEO of Renaissance, Frank Del Rio. He regrouped after September 11th, declared bankruptcy, sold off some of the ships, and started Oceania.

These ships are smaller in size (they hold about 700 passengers), and lend themselves to providing a more service-intensive experience.

It was very interesting one weekend when I had the opportunity to tour the *Pacific Princess* and one of the Oceania ships on the same day…. Oceania has put a considerable amount of money into refurbishing the ship, and the difference was quite evident. The room appointments are more luxurious, and the public areas more sumptuous in their fabrics, design, and furniture. For example, in the buffet area, Princess had plastic tables and chairs, whereas Oceania had teak. Princess kept the fabric and furnishings from the Renaissance days, and Oceania completely replaced them.

That's not to say Princess' small ship experience is not exceptional; it is, but the price is certainly more expensive on these Premium lines, so it depends on what your client is used to.

Both cruise lines offer complementary bottled water, soft drinks, specialty coffees and teas, and wines poured at lunch and dinner. Azamara offers select standard spirits as well.

Oceania still has tipping, so that is an important consideration to advise your clients…however, the service is impeccable and the ships are truly beautiful, so hopefully that will make up for the extra $16 per person, per day, that is recommended for tipping. ($23 per person, per day, for Suites.) Azamara includes gratuities in their cruise fare.

Be sure to book early, as these cruise lines typically have two-for-one specials if you book during the year prior to the voyage. If you are part of a host agency and they are part of a consortium, you can sometimes get tipping and onboard credits included for your clients as well.

Cunard Cruise Line
www.cunard.com

Cunard is a cruise line unto itself. It's not Mass Market, but is somewhere between Premium and Luxury. You may recall the *QEII*, that venerable old ocean liner that plied the Atlantic Ocean, traveling back and forth from New York to Southampton. Well, there is a new *Queen Elizabeth* making her way between the old world and new, and she is as elegant and grand as her predecessor.

Cunard is as "old English" as it comes. There is definitely a class-system on board, and woe to he or she who deigns to cross the line!

The suites and mini suites, called Queen's Grill and Princess Grill suites, have their own dining rooms, and these passengers are considered to be the first-class passengers. Their dining rooms are in an area that is not accessible to the Britannia Restaurant passengers. Mind you, the Britannia Restaurant is absolutely lovely, and the food suitable, so it really is a matter of perception. There is also a club lounge for the first-class passengers, and they guard the doors with the ferocity of a three-headed dog on the banks of the River Styx!

The ships of Cunard are the *Queen Elizabeth*, *Queen Mary*, and *Queen Victoria*. These ships are lovely, with wood-paneled libraries, elegant public rooms, and the Royal Academy of Dramatic Arts onboard as entertainment. Todd English has his own restaurant, and there is an observatory on the *Queen Mary*, quite unlike anything I have ever seen at sea, complete with a high powered telescope and astronomer onboard giving lectures.

Cunard caters to a very specific passenger: one who appreciates dressing for dinner and elegance throughout the voyage. Please be sure to qualify your clients if you choose to book them on Cunard. For those who appreciate this type of cruising experience, Cunard can be a trip of a lifetime. I can't imagine a more elegant way to travel from New York to England!

Viking Cruises

The newest player in the Premium Cruise world is Viking Cruises, the sister of Viking River Cruises. And, what a splash they have made in the cruise industry! Their ships are absolutely gorgeous, with 930 guests, and their suites range from 270 to 1163 square feet. All suites have verandahs, and have premium amenities, including large bathrooms with double sinks and heated floors.

Viking includes one shore excursion in every port of call, which can really save your clients money. There's unlimited free Wi-Fi, multiple dining venues, beer, wine and soft drinks with onboard lunch and dinner, twenty-four-hour specialty coffees, teas and bottled water, self-service launderette, and twenty-four-hour room service.

My clients who have cruised Viking have absolutely raved about them! The service is impeccable, and the ships are state of the art. They currently have seven ships sailing, with more planned.

If your clients aren't quite ready for the expense of a Luxury Cruise, but want a similar experience to Luxury, Viking is the way to go. I would even go so far as to include them in with the Luxury Cruise Lines, but the thing that holds them back from this categorization is that they are not as all-inclusive as all of the other Luxury Cruise Lines. You have to pay for alcohol and gratuities.

Viking can be expensive, but make sure to book as far in advance as possible, because you can sometimes get two-for-one deals or other discounts when you book early.

LUXURY CRUISE LINES

Crystal Cruises, Regent Seven Seas, Seabourn, and Silverseas

The above cruise lines represent the top of the line in cruising. Most are all-inclusive, which means your client will pay a much higher price for their cruise fare, but everything is included, including gratuities, alcohol, all beverages, and in the case of Regent Seven Seas, basic shore excursions.

Their ships are typically small, with a higher passenger-to-staff ratio.

Sometimes I have found that it is less expensive to cruise on one of these cruise lines, with all that is included, than on a Mass Market ship; usually this is when the passengers tend to imbibe a larger amount of alcohol during their day. Just think: fruity drinks around the pool during the day, pre-dinner cocktails in the lounge with hors d'oeuvres, wine with each course at dinner, and an after-dinner aperitif. This all adds up to quite a bit on a daily basis. Throw in their soft drinks and bottled water, and you can see how this can add up! (Disney Cruise Line, for example, charges $35 for a case of bottled water! This is the same case that costs $3.50 in the grocery store at home.)

If your clients are more mature and might appreciate a Luxury cruise line experience, it might behoove you to do some price comparisons between one of these cruise lines and a Premium or Mass Market ship – especially when you consider shore excursions are included with Regent Seven Seas. (These are very basic shore excursions; city tours in most places, which are good for first time visitors to the ports. Other shore excursions that are more elaborate are of course for sale onboard the ship. Make sure to check with the cruise line to see what exactly is offered and if it meets the needs of your clients.)

Children are *not* encouraged on these Premium or Luxury cruise lines, so these ships would not be appropriate for family cruising.

The only one that might make an exception is Crystal Cruises during the summer months and holiday sailings, but even then, there are no dedicated children's playrooms.

The crowd for Premium and Luxury cruising is decidedly older and more mature; you will occasionally find the young entrepreneur who enjoys a more up-market traveling experience, but this is not the norm. The cruises are typically longer in duration, so the crowd is usually retired or self-employed.

Service is the hallmark of these cruise lines, and their staff is paid accordingly. There is no nickel-and-diming for gratuities, and it makes a nice change to have the level of service where your needs are anticipated. A smaller ship means the staff gets to know you and your desires, thus heightening the feeling of intimacy on these ships.

Just remember these experiences are for a certain type of client. Just because your passengers might be wealthy does not mean they will enjoy this type of cruise; if they are partiers, these ships are definitely *not* what they are looking for! Remember to always match your client to their cruise line and ship. You can learn more about how to do this in CLIA's training courses.

River Cruising

The newest trend in cruising these days is river cruising. Thanks to the aggressive television advertising campaign of Viking River Cruises, river cruising has now come to the forefront of the traveling public's mind as an alternative to the huge ocean cruise ships, especially in Europe.

We've long had paddleboats plying the Mississippi River, and those are still a viable product in the United States, but the real focus has been river cruising in Europe, most especially along the Rhine and Danube rivers.

The most popular cruises, according to Avalon Waterways and Viking River Cruises, are the eight-day introduction cruises of these two rivers. With that in mind, these two cruises have the most departures and choices of ships being offered.

Other rivers that are offered are

- Rivers of France, including the Seine, Garonne, Saone, Gironde, Dordogne, and Rhone
- Waterways of Belgium and Holland, especially in the spring for Tulip Time Cruises
- Moselle River which flows through France, Luxembourg and Germany
- Main River and Elbe Rivers in Germany and Czech Republic

- Douro River in Portugal
- Po River in Italy

And in other parts of the world, there are

- Russian Rivers, including the Volga, Neva, Svir, and other waterways in Russia
- Yangtze River, including Three Gorges in China
- Mekong River from China to Viet Nam
- Irrawaddy River in Myanmar
- Galapagos Islands
- Nile River in Egypt
- Ganges River in India

European river cruising tends to offer similar amenities onboard the ships, with some cruise lines offering a more all-inclusive experience. All of the cruise lines offer the following:

- Wine, beer and soft drinks with lunch and dinner, and sparkling wine with breakfast
- Escorted tours in each port with local guides and individual listening devices
- Bottled water in the stateroom and sometimes on tour
- Free Wi-Fi (on most ships)
- Outside staterooms with a variety of balcony choices
- Premium bath products in the bathrooms
- A professional cruise director who handles all of the different aspects of the cruise, including port talks, and arranging the tours in each port.
- English-speaking staff
- Transfers to and from the airport if you take their air program and arrive or depart on the day of embarkation or disembarkation (otherwise there may be a charge)
- Bicycles in port for the guests use (on some cruises)

Then, some offer a more all-inclusive experience with the following:

- Gratuities paid to all staff, including shipboard and shoreside
- All beverages included twenty-four hours a day, not just at mealtimes
- A variety of shore excursions to choose from, including those considered "optional" by other cruise lines

The staterooms vary, from large suites, rooms with balconies, rooms with French balconies, and standard rooms. (A French-balcony is basically a sliding glass door that opens up with a balcony rail in front of it. There is no space to step out, per se, but the glass door opens to give a balcony feel.) The standard rooms are found on the bottom passenger deck. They have small windows at the level of the river; the windows don't really have a view because they are so close to the river, but they do let in natural sunlight. In my personal experience, these staterooms are claustrophobic in the way inside staterooms are on ocean cruises. I try to encourage my clients to stay away from these standard staterooms and at least upgrade to the first available stateroom category on the middle passenger deck.

Most ships have three passenger decks. The suites and balcony staterooms (both regular and French) are found on the top two passenger decks, with the standard staterooms on the bottom passenger deck. This bottom deck is actually partly under the river water, so you can sometimes hear water noises when you're trying to sleep, if the ship is sailing throughout the night. You can also sometimes hear the locks on the river if you are passing through locks during the night. Like I said, I try to discourage this category of staterooms.

There are all classes of river cruise ships, from which I would term *Premium* to *Ultra-Luxury*.

ULTRA-LUXURY RIVER CRUISING

Crystal River Cruises

Capping off the ultra-luxury cruises would be Crystal Cruises' new ships, which debuted in 2017 and 2018. Their first ship is the *Crystal Mozart*, and is indicative of the future of Crystal River Cruises. The *Crystal Mozart* is twice as large and twice as wide as any riverboat sailing European waterways. There are four dining venues, a spa and fitness center, and an array of high-tech features in their suites, including bathrooms boasting heated towel racks and TOTO Washlet systems with a heated toilet seat that opens and closes automatically, as well as iPad directories found in each stateroom. Their suites also include butler service, which is a step above the typical room steward found on other river cruises. The cuisine is from celebrated chefs, with possible restaurant experiences at Michelin-starred or highly renowned local restaurants.

Crystal has also come out with four sister ships plying the rivers of Europe: *Crystal Bach, Crystal Debussy, Crystal Mahler* and *Crystal Ravel.* These are also beautifully appointed with suites that range from 759 square feet down to petite suites that are 188 square feet. Each ship holds 106 guests, and also has butler service.

Crystal is an all-inclusive product, and includes all of your shore excursions, the afore mentioned butler service, unlimited soft drinks and bottled water en-suite, Nespresso or Inspresso coffee machines, twenty-four-hour room service, complementary self-service laundry, unlimited fine wines, champagnes and premium spirits and beers, plus a Crystal Signature Event on each itinerary. Crystal also has luxury motor coaches in each destination featuring complimentary Wi-Fi. Some even offer epicurean experiences at Michelin-starred or highly acclaimed local restaurants in select destinations and a curated Crystal Collection shore excursion.

Crystal embodies luxury and elegance to the highest standard and is perfect for your more affluent clients.

Uniworld Boutique River Cruise Collection

I have to say, Uniworld has the most beautifully decorated ships out there, with the designer of Red Carnation Hotels also designing each and every Uniworld ship. Each stateroom is different, and each ship has its own character and flair. Uniworld also has butler service for their suites, and all the amenities of an all-inclusive cruise line, including gratuities (even for your butler!), *all* of your shore excursions, including the following:

optional excursions that other cruise lines might charge for

- all of your beverages, including premium brands
- concierge services
- 24-hour room service
- exercise classes
- exclusive events, such as an evening in St. Mark's Basilica in Venice, Italy where Uniworld guests are the only people in the church at the time

They have specialized shore excursions, called Do As the Locals Do, where guests go in-depth at the port of call, not just the typical tourist sightseeing, but immersing themselves in the lives of local citizens, from exploring favorite meeting places to tasting beloved regional foods. Uniworld prides itself on using local ingredients in their cuisine, with farm-to-table foods sourced from regional farms, farmers markets, and artisanal producers. It's not uncommon to see the chef shopping at the local farmers market in town for that night's dinner.

Uniworld's staterooms come in a wide variety of sizes. The smallest can be found on the River Ambassador and River Baroness. They measure 128 to 130 square feet. And the smallest suites on the River Baroness, River Countess, River Duchess, River Princess, River Queen, and River

Royale measure between 214 and 217 square feet. The newer ships have the largest staterooms, with those on the S.S. Catherine and S.S. Maria Theresa measuring between 162 and 410 square feet. The most common stateroom size is almost 200 square feet.

Uniworld offers several family-friendly departures on their various itineraries and on certain sailings, and encourages families to travel together, with kid-friendly menus and shore excursions specially designed for each itinerary. There are language classes, dessert-making classes with the ship's pastry chef, and hands-on-craft workshops for the kids. There's even a dedicated Family Host to oversee the young traveler's activities.

Uniworld's Serenity River Spa has a fully equipped fitness center, and even a heated pool on some of their ships. There are onboard yoga classes, exercise classes, a certified onboard wellness instructor, complimentary bicycles and Nordic Walking Sticks, and even a Traveling Lite menu and vegetarian meal options. You can choose your level of activity for your shore excursions, from Gentle Walking tours to Go Active tours for those who want a more active experience. In short, Uniworld provides an exceptional cruising experience, both onboard and ashore.

LUXURY ALL-INCLUSIVE CRUISING

Scenic

One of the river cruise lines that is trying to break into the North American market is Scenic Cruises. They are considered an All-Inclusive cruise line because beverages are included throughout the day, as well as gratuities, excursions, and all of the amenities listed above. Scenic also has butlers, and includes complimentary laundry service as part of their offerings. Their balcony rooms are unique in that they have a large window that opens up from the top and lowers down, so that you have an open-air balcony, called a Sun Lounge, within your stateroom. Their ships are called Space-Ships and include a wellness area and gym, and casual all-day dining at their River Café.

One of their unique offerings is in port with their Tailormade GPS Guided Tours. This is available in more than 140 locations, and allows the guest to experience the port at their own pace using a range of directional-guided GPS tours. These start and end at the ship, so the guests never get lost.

Transfers are included at no extra charge, no matter when the guest arrives. Scenic will oftentimes have special rates on their airfare, so it pays to check their airfare costs first before trying to book air separately.

Scenic is part of a travel company that has been in business for thirty years, starting with coach tours along Australia's Great Ocean Road. They pride themselves in their all-inclusive product, and their trademark phrase is that they go to "the nth degree" when it comes to their passengers. They offer a Scenic river cruise guarantee for your client's peace of mind. It is definitely worth checking out this cruise line if you are looking for a luxury all-inclusive experience.

Tauck River Cruises

Tauck is another luxury river cruise company that boasts an all-inclusive experience. Again, unlimited complimentary beverages, pillow-topped mattresses, 400 thread count bed linens, luxury toiletries, in-room movies, and a stocked mini-bar. Gratuities are included for all staff, and Tauck actually has not only a cruise director, but also three Tauck Directors, all professional employees of Tauck. Personal expenses, however, are not included, such as phone calls, room service, top-shelf alcohol and specialty wines, laundry, and other optional extras.

Tauck's staterooms vary in size, from 150 square feet up to 300 square feet for their Category 7s. The rooms mostly have French balconies, and all Category 7s are triples with a pull-out sleeping couch...perfect for families!

Speaking of families, Tauck has an excellent program called Bridges. Tauck Bridges river cruises are designed for learning, doing, and playing together as a family. They have special programs just for kids (children must be at least eight years old) and special itineraries in place just for families. There is even a price reduction for children under the age of twelve.

Other All-Inclusive Luxury River Cruise Lines

- A-Rosa
- CroisiEurope

PREMIUM RIVER CRUISE LINES

With Premium River Cruise Lines, many of the same things are offered by each company: shore excursions in each port; wine, beer, and soft drinks with lunch and dinner, and sparkling wine with breakfast; free Wi-Fi; bicycles for guests to ride in each port; special hands-free listening devices to use on shore excursions; bottled water; luxury bath products in the bathroom as well as deluxe linens and towels; transfers (if you take their air program, and on the dates the cruise begins and ends); all of your meals (even in specialty restaurants); and gourmet coffees and teas throughout the day.

What is not included are things such as gratuities, laundry, telephone, minibar, alcohol, beverages not during lunch or dinner, optional excursions (in addition to those offered in each port), any meals not specified in the itinerary at hotels either prior to or after the cruise, and any items of a personal nature. (This is just a list of those that come to mind. Each cruise line may be different, but this is a good indication of what is not included.)

Avalon Waterways

Avalon Waterways is part of the Globus Family of Brands. They currently have ships in Europe, and also cruise to the Yangtze River,

Mekong and Irrawaddy rivers, Nile River, and in South America to the Peruvian Amazon and Galapagos.

Avalon does an excellent job with their attention to detail. The cruise director is onboard to make sure everything runs smoothly, and is a consummate professional with what they do. On my Avalon Waterways cruise, the river in France was too high, so we had to disembark two days early. The cruise director made sure we were taken care of: they booked the entire ship's company into a first class deluxe hotel in Paris, provided all of our meals, and even threw in the Versailles Shore Excursion for free for every single passenger as an apology for inconveniencing us. It wasn't their fault the river was too high, but they made sure our holiday wasn't ruined by crossing every T and dotting every I. We were always kept abreast of what was going on, and Avalon turned what would have been a disaster into a lovely way to end our trip.

Avalon's claim to fame is their view…on all of their European ships, they have positioned the beds so they face the window. There's nothing like lying on your bed watching the view of the river going by! Their sliding glass doors are eleven feet wide, and open up nine feet so that you can create your own Panorama Open Air Balcony in your stateroom. Basically, Avalon does not have balconies that you step out on…by opening up the sliding glass door, your stateroom actually becomes your balcony, with a sitting area right in front of the windows. So, you can feel like you are outside, but with the comfort of the stateroom ceiling over you to protect from the elements. On these ships, the average suite is 200 square feet, with a very large bathroom considering you are on a river cruise. They feature Comfort Collection Beds with memory foam toppers; Egyptian super-combed cotton linens; and a choice of pillows, bathrobes, and slippers for your use on the ship; and have Continental breakfast room service available.

Avalon prides themselves on their new food program, Avalon Fresh. Created with two of the rising stars in the European Culinary world, the Wrenkh brothers, Avalon Fresh allows guests to indulge in creative dishes that are surprisingly healthy and flavorful. Their philosophy is to procure the freshest ingredients from local farmers, to give passengers a true farm-to-table experience.

There are also Active Discovery cruises. These special itineraries give guests the option of experiencing the ports in a more active way, whether it's bicycling, or canoeing, or engaging with your hosts in the most active, engaged, and fun ways possible. Of course, you don't have to take part in these activities and can just experience the cruise at a more leisurely pace. It's up to the guest.

As far as their Irrawaddy River cruises, Avalon Waterways is the only cruise line that has a ship that goes north 200 miles more on the Irrawaddy than any other cruise ship… This way, passengers are on the ship for more of the sightseeing. This sets them apart from other cruise lines that cannot go up that high on the river. Their ship is just beautiful, with eighteen suites that measure 245 square feet. This ship also has the Open-Air Balcony feature similar to the European Ships.

One thing to note: the minimum age allowed on Avalon is eight years old. They really don't encourage children onboard Avalon Waterways cruises, as there are no children's facilities or special programs for them. There are also no triple staterooms, only doubles.

Viking River Cruises

Ah, yes, the biggest player in the river cruise market! There are so many ships that not even my sales rep knows all the names of the Longships! Viking River has done a wonderful job of bringing river cruising to the minds of travelers the world over. They have engaged in a vigorous advertising campaign, and I think the river cruise business is all the better for it.

Viking River Cruises' Longships have been voted Best River Cruise Ships by Cruise Critic and also in 2014 by Condé Nast. They have an innovative setup with one side of the ship with full balconies and the other side of the ship with French balconies. The full balconied rooms are 205 square feet (with the balcony) and the French-balconied rooms are 135 square feet. There are also Veranda Suites that are 275 square feet and Explorer Suites that are 445 square feet. And we can't forget the standard staterooms with the small windows, which are 150 square feet.

They also have a number of other ships that sail in Europe, with size depending on the rivers they are sailing on. For example, the *Viking Hemming*, *Viking Torgil*, and *Viking Osfrid* were specifically built to cruise Portugal's Douro River. There are a number of other ships, so when you book Viking River Cruises, make sure whether you are booking a Longship or not.

Viking River Cruises is great at offering two-for-one fares with up-to-free airfare, so you want to encourage your clients to book during this promotion period. You will want to keep abreast of their offers, so I recommend subscribing to their e-mails so you can be advised of what is in the marketplace. (As a matter of fact, you might want to subscribe to all of the river cruise companies you think you will do business with. It's always good to know what is being offered so you can compare and contrast the different prices for your clients.)

Viking River also cruises the waterways of Russia, Southeast Asia, and Egypt.

One thing to note: the minimum age for passengers is eighteen years old. They are not set up for children, nor do they encourage children on their sailings.

FAMILIES ON RIVER CRUISES

Are river cruises the best choice for families with children? Only if you book a specific sailing that is tailored to families with small children (see AMAWaterways, Uniworld, and Tauck).

Each cruise line has their own specifications about minimum age and what they offer. With all of them, children eighteen and younger must be supervised at all times by an adult who is twenty-one years or older.

Probably the best out there now is AMAWaterways' partnership with Adventures by Disney. Adventures by Disney now has river cruises set up just for families (children must be six and older, with recommended age of eight and older) and they have triple accommodations, unlike many of the other river cruise companies. As of this printing, they are offering Danube and Rhine River Cruises. Disney thinks of everything and keeps the families busy from sunup to sundown. There's all kinds of activities just for kids, (too many to list here) and the ports are storybook beautiful. If I wanted to take a river cruise with my family, this is the way I would do it: with an Adventures by Disney River Cruise.

As I mentioned previously, Uniworld has a family-friendly program called Generations. They encourage multi-generational travel, with four being the minimum age required (although the recommended minimum age is eight). As of this printing, there are thirteen different departures on eight different itineraries. They offer 50% savings off the cruise-only fare for children aged four to eighteen years old when traveling with an adult. There are kid-friendly menus with unlimited beverages onboard, complimentary bicycles and helmets for use onshore, exciting family-friendly shore excursions specially designed for each itinerary, language classes, dessert making with the ship's pastry chef, hands-on craft workshops including Venetian art and more, and most important, a dedicated family host to oversee the children's activities.

Tauck Bridges sailings are also set up with families in mind. They offer more itineraries, including not only the Rhine and Danube, but also the Seine to Normandy (what a great way to learn about WWII) and the Rhone River in France. Tauck has special Bridges Tour Directors who specialize in working with families. Like Uniworld, everything is included, including all beverages and gratuities. Make sure when you are booking children on Tauck River Cruises that it is a specific Tauck Bridges sailing. The minimum age to cruise is four years as well.

A-Rosa River Cruise Line accepts children aged two and older. There are no special programs for children, but they sometimes have special rates for kids if traveling with an adult.

As mentioned above, Avalon Waterways has a minimum age requirement of eight years old, and there are no triple staterooms available.

CroisiEurope River Cruises actually allows children of all ages to cruise! Even though infants can cruise, there is no special food or accommodation made for them onboard. Passengers will have to bring their own Pack'n'Play or other type of crib for the child to sleep in. The cruise line does have triple staterooms, so children can share a cabin with their parents at a reduced cost.

And finally, children must be twelve years of age to travel on Emerald Waterways, Viking River Cruises, and Scenic Cruises. These do not have any special programs for children, or even discounted fares.

NORTH AMERICAN RIVER CRUISES

I'm sure you are familiar with the picture of a paddle wheeler sailing down the Mississippi River. Yes, those ships still ply those waters, and the Mississippi is still a very viable offering in the river cruise market.

The other area in North America that sees some action is the Pacific Northwest. There, we find the Columbia, Snake and, Willamette Rivers. But first, the Mississippi and the deep South…

One of the most recognized American River Cruise Company is American Queen Steamboat Company. They have four ships: the *American Queen*, the *American Empres*s, the *American Countess*, and the new *American Duchess*, the first all-suite US river cruise vessel. The *American Queen* and *American Empress* are both member vessels of the Historic Hotels of America. The *American Queen* carries about 400 guests and the *American Empress* carries slightly more than 200 guests. The *American Countess* sails on the Tennessee, Ohio, Cumberland and Mississippi Rivers. Both are paddle wheelers, and the *American Queen* has the largest collection of Tiffany glass in existence. The *American Duchess* carries 166 guests, so half the size of *American Queen*, but with the largest accommodations in every cabin category level on the river. She is the first purpose-built, all-suite, boutique paddle wheeler, and has everything from Verandah Suites of 240 to 330 square feet to Loft Suites of 550 square feet, to Owner's Suites, also 550 square feet.

The *American Queen* and *American Duchess* sail the Mississippi River, and the *American Empress* sails in the Pacific Northwest. According to American Queen Steamboat Company, the main attraction on any of their cruises is the award-winning shore excursions. They have signature Hop-On-Hop-Off guided excursions, which allow guests the freedom of choosing their own path in the great cities they visit. Passengers receive a map with the Hop-On-Hop-Off tour route and its numbered stops. Attractions with a gold star include admission just by the guest showing their cruise ID. They have deluxe motorcoaches whereby passengers can board at the dock and enjoy a locally narrated tour throughout each port of call. Guests hop off wherever they want because another motorcoach is on its way to pick them up and continue the historical narration of their river port city. Motorcoaches typically stop every fifteen to twenty minutes. American Queen Steamboat Company also has Premium Shore Excursions that offer guests the opportunity to delve even deeper into their specific interests. They are available for purchase and provide comprehensive, in-depth, and rare experiences. Guests can go online to explore their Premium Shore Excursions prior to their cruise.

Like with European River Cruises, complementary wine and beer are with dinner, as well as cappuccinos, espressos, bottled water, and soft drinks throughout the voyage. The ships have a country-club casual ambiance, so no formalwear is required. There are daily lectures by their "Riverlorian," the onboard history and culture expert, and there is entertainment at night, including revues, cabaret, jazz and blues, and a six-piece orchestra.

The final North American river-cruise line is American Cruise Lines. They have two paddle-wheel riverboats, the *Queen of the Mississippi* (2015) and *America* (2016). These ships cruise the Mississippi, Ohio, and Cumberland rivers. They also have a number of other ships cruising New England, the Pacific Northwest, the Southeastern part of America, and even Alaska. They boast thirty-five cruise itineraries to twenty-eight states...that's quite a wide breadth of cruises to choose from in the United States.

American Cruise Line offers a range of music entertainment, from jazz to rock and roll. They also have local experts, as well as Riverlorians who come onboard to give passengers the history and culture of what they are seeing. Their informal lectures, open discussions, and activities bring local history, nature, and culture to life through their knowledge and passion for American heritage.

Each evening before dinner, there is a complimentary cocktail hour offering drinks and hors d'ouevres. Wine and beer are served with meals. An array of shore excursions are also complimentary. There is an all-American crew onboard, with ships built in America. They boast exquisite cuisine from their highly trained chefs, and offer a relaxed atmosphere onboard.

Now, on to some of their ships:

The *American Constellation* is a small ship that sails to New England, the Hudson River, and the southeastern part of America. It's their brand new (2017) 175-passenger ship and is uniquely designed to navigate the inland waterways of the East Coast. The staterooms are large and spacious (450 square feet for the Owner's Suite to 226 square feet for a single stateroom; most staterooms with private balconies are 350 square feet, and outside staterooms run from 260 to 302 square feet) and there are full-sized bathrooms for most of the categories of cabins. There are two wheelchair-accessible staterooms and an elevator that spans all of the passenger decks.

The *American Pride* is a 150-passenger paddle wheeler that sails the Columbia and Snake rivers in the Pacific Northwest. The staterooms are also large and spacious, with balcony rooms at 304 square feet and ocean view staterooms at 290 square feet. This ship also has single traveler accommodations, with a private balcony room at 230 square feet and ocean-view staterooms at 203 square feet. The bathrooms are hotel-sized with all the needed amenities. The ship boasts laundry facilities as well as an elevator that travels to all passenger decks. There is one handicapped-accessible room on this ship as well.

The *American Spirit* (built in 2005) is a 100-passenger cruise ship that sails Alaska and the Pacific Northwest. Itineraries include Puget Sound and the San Juan Islands, as well as various Alaska cruises. The Owner's Suite is 350 square feet, with balcony rooms ranging from 263 to 283 square feet. Ocean-view staterooms are 258 square feet, and single balcony rooms are 248 square feet. There is also one handicapped-accessible stateroom on this ship.

The *American Star* (built in 2007) is also a 100-passenger cruise ship that plies New England, the Hudson River, and the southeast. It is a sister ship to the *American Spirit* and has the same accommodations. Both ships also have hotel-sized bathrooms and satellite TV and DVD player in each stateroom.

Another sister ship is the *Independence*, which also sails the Hudson River, New England, and the southeast. She was built in 2010 and boasts the same stateroom sizes as her sisters, the *American Spirit* and *American Star*.

Then there's the *Queen of the West*, a paddle wheeler built in 1995, but refurbished in 2011 for 120 passengers. She cruises the Columbia and Snake rivers. Her Owner's Suites are 280 square feet with a very large balcony for staterooms up on the top deck. The balcony staterooms have 236 to 246 square feet of space, with the outside staterooms at 183 to 204 square feet. There are also singles with private balconies at 181 square feet, and singles with picture windows at 149 square feet.

Another new ship the *American Constitution*, cruising New England, the Hudson River, and the southeast. She will have 175 passengers and the latest in technology and modern design. There will be adjoining staterooms—perfect for families—and two handicapped-accessible staterooms. This ship will have complimentary Wi-Fi, laundry service, and even room service at breakfast. The staterooms range in size, with the Owner's Suites at more than 450 square feet and Verandah Suites also at 450 square feet, to balcony staterooms at 350 square feet, window staterooms between 260 to 302 square feet, and finally singles at 226 to 250 square feet, some with private balconies. Like most of the American Cruise Line–built ships, there are hotel-sized bathrooms with all the top amenities, and the *Constitution* will have a grand dining room that will accommodate all guests at a single sitting.

2020 has new riverboats coming to American Cruise Lines: *American Jazz*, *American Harmony*, *American Song*, and *American Melody*. Check their website for the latest ship news and itineraries.

So, hopefully this has given you some insight into river cruising. It's the fastest growing sector in my personal business, and the commissions are fantastic! It will behoove you to order brochures for all of the river cruise companies explained above, and pour over them.... Learn the ins and outs of each company. This way, when one of your clients asks you about them, you will be ready to go. Also, if you need to boost your business, contact all of your ocean cruise passengers you have booked in the past in balcony, suite, and mini-suite staterooms and talk to them about the possibility of a river cruise.

And most of all, get yourself on a river cruise as soon as you can. This is a very specific product and is nothing like an ocean cruise... once you've experienced it for yourself, you will be able to show the enthusiasm for it that will excite your clients. I love this product, and my sales show it. Now it is *your* turn to try one!

Commission

As TRAVEL AGENTS, WE MAKE our money from the suppliers we sell. Some travel agents charge a booking fee, something that is becoming more common. I have considered doing so, but the competition is so steep out there for business that I will only do so if it is for a large group of people that requires a lot of research prior to booking. I will usually apply the research fee to their payment once they decide to book. A good example of this would be a wedding party that needs research for the reception, wedding site, etc., in addition to their cruise. I once made the mistake of planning a wedding for a client, complete with the wedding, reception in one of the ports, transportation for fifty guests to and from the ship, cruises for every guest (most of them had never cruised, nor even owned a credit card), flowers, the list goes on.... I spent more than seventy-two hours researching, booking, etc. A few months after booking, the groom was deployed to Afghanistan, they had to cancel their big wedding cruise, and they settled for getting married at home with a judge presiding. I did not receive a single penny for all my work, and I just didn't feel right asking the bride to pay me anything when I had not arranged for a research fee in advance. (Her husband was going to defend our country! I felt that was probably payment enough for me.)

How much would you charge? I ask for a $100 research fee in advance for a group like this. This is very reasonable when you consider how much a wedding planner charges for her services. After all, you are, in essence, a wedding planner in situations like this. **Plus, for all cruise bookings I make, I now charge a $50 per person cancellation fee if they cancel.** I make this very clear in my correspondence to them, as well as in their Reservation Authorization that they sign and send back to me. These forms and letters will be in the appendix of the book, and I encourage you to personalize them for yourself and send them out when your clients book cruises. This simply protects you in your business. (More about these forms later on in the book.) I think it is very reasonable to expect a $50 cancellation fee, because you have put hours of work into researching the best cruise for them, booking it, and then processing all the forms and payments.

That being said, I usually forgo the fee for my best clients; these are the people who cruise every year and stick with me as their travel agent. I know that when they cancel, they will make it up to me in a future cruise sale. I will also forgo the fee if they cancel and rebook immediately, because I eventually get the commission, just not on the original cruise sale. It is completely up to you; remember, this is *your* business, so you need to feel comfortable with the decision to charge or not charge a fee.

So, how do commissions work? The typical commission rate is 10%. Then, the more you sell per year, your commission may go up; for the most part, cruise lines go up to 15-16%. How do you get the higher commission? Sell that cruise line! It's not uncommon to make 16% on one or two cruise lines, 12% on a few more, and then 10% on the rest. How do you get the highest commission amount for every cruise line? You join a host agency. Host agencies can have hundreds of agents all selling under the same CLIA or IATA number, so their volume warrants the larger commission structures. I make more earning a percentage through my host agency than I did earning a full commission on my own, so joining a host agency was a wise move for me.

Commissions are paid typically on the cruise fare, but not the port taxes (Non-Commissionable Fares) or government fees. They may also pay 10% on hotels, transfers, and insurance sold through the cruise line. Some will pay a commission on airfare that is booked through them; this is worth looking into, as most airlines do not pay any commission on air booked directly through airlines, so this may be a way to earn commission on an element of the cruise trip on which you would otherwise not earn anything. (Please see information on air tickets found on page 59).

Cruise lines pay commission in one of two ways: Soon after you have made final payment for the cruise, or not until after the passenger has sailed. Payments can sometimes take up to three weeks after sailing date to get to you. If you are a member of a host agency, commissions are usually paid in the month after your passenger has sailed. This ensures there is no commission "recall" if the passenger cancels. If commission is paid soon after final payment and your passenger cancels, you may receive a commission "recall" notice that requires you to re-pay the commission back to the cruise line or passenger. If the passenger has taken the insurance policy through the cruise line, your commission may be "protected," which means you get to keep the commission even though the clients receive a full refund. Every cruise line is different, so you will need to check with that cruise line to see their policy. (This has nothing to do with the $50 cancellation fee I spoke about earlier; this fee would go into effect if there was a commission "recall" and I did not receive any compensation for my work.) I've received commission checks for as little as $19 for a two-day coastal voyage, to over $15,000 for a world cruise. It just depends on the cost of the voyage.

Making a Cruise Booking

So, you've talked to your client, and you have determined where they want to go and what cruise line they want to sail on. Let's take, for example, a Princess Cruise to the Caribbean. How do you go about booking it?

There are typically two ways to book cruises: On the phone with a cruise reservation agent, or online. Most cruise lines have online websites for travel agents; these have revolutionized how travel agents can do business, because now you have access twenty-four hours a day, seven days a week to the actual inventory of staterooms on any given sailing date! I actually do most of my reservations in the wee hours of the morning and on weekends, so I can spend the daylight hours on the phone selling and taking care of my clients.

If you are an experienced air agent, you may have access to a Global Distribution system (GDS), and your agency may require you to make bookings through that portal. For the purpose of this book, I will not be referencing GDS, as the majority of new cruise agents are working from home and have only Internet access.

If you are not Internet savvy, you can always pick up the phone to call the cruise line. I find it more efficient to use the Internet programs, so we will discuss the steps you will take booking online.

Elements of a Cruise Booking

There are many parts of each booking; no longer is there just a single cruise fare that encompasses all charges. Cruise lines have taken to breaking out each element of the fare to show the passenger the individual port taxes and government fees. Let's look at each of these.

Cruise Fare

This is the actual amount the cruise line makes for the passenger sailing on their ship. Some cruise lines include the Port Tax (also called Non-Commissionable Fare, or NCF) in the quoted price, but show what that amount is in the recap of the cruise booking.

Port Tax or Non-Commissionable Fare

As mentioned above, Port Tax or NCFs are charged by the cruise line to cover taxes levied from each individual port, per passenger. On World Cruises this can be as high as $2500 because of the number of ports visited. American ports tend to charge more than, say, Caribbean ports, so the port taxes for Alaska tend to be quite high. Cruise lines might also add a little bit more handling fee in these taxes, so they may not be exactly the amount the ports are levying per passenger; there is a cap, however, on this. The separating-out of Port Taxes caused quite a stir in the travel agent community when they first separated them, because in the past, travel agents were paid commission on the entire amount. Now, most cruise lines do not pay any commission on the Port Taxes.

Government Fees

In addition to port taxes, there may be government fees levied by the government of each country visited. These are collected in this charge, and again, are not commissionable.

Transfers

Transfers are the transportation from the airport to the ship prior to the voyage, and from the ship to the airport post-cruise. I strongly recommend my clients take the cruise line's transfers if they are arriving on the day of sailing in every port with the exception of Fort Lauderdale. (The Fort Lauderdale airport is only about ten minutes away from the port, so they can often get transfers via taxi for far less than the ship's transfers, especially if there are more than two passengers). In places like Whittier and Seward (Alaska), Venice (Italy), and a host of other port cities, the ships are hard to get to, and it is so nice having those uniformed cruise line representatives in the baggage claim area taking care of tired, bedraggled travelers who just want to get to their ship after a long day of travel. The passengers must claim their luggage from the airline, identify it as their own, and hand it over to the cruise representative, who is usually standing right outside of baggage claim with a clipboard showing the cruise line's name and logo. You will have to call in (or enter online) their air schedule, so the cruise line knows which airline, flight, and time of arrival to expect them. You will also have to enter the information for post-cruise transfers so they know how many buses they need at any given time to get your passengers to the airport on time for their flight. There is a cost for each way, so you can also book only pre-cruise or post-cruise if you wish. If your clients are booking a hotel package, transfers are sometimes provided as part of the cost; please see HOTELS below.

Airfare

In the past, cruise lines included air fare in the cost of the cruise from most major U.S. air cities to the port of departure. As the ship capacities have grown, the demand for the limited number of air tickets into any given port city has grown as well, and the cruise lines had to spend a disproportionate amount of time trying to negotiate air contracts in order to meet the demand. As the airline industry has changed over the years, cruise lines realized they needed to concentrate on selling cruises, and not spend all their time and resources on finding air tickets for every single passenger, so they have made air a completely separate component of the cruise. Travel agents also realized that they were able to find much lower air fare online (i.e., with Southwest or other low-cost carriers), or with their own agencies' air contracts with major airlines.

Rule of thumb with doing your own air flights: Prior to the cruise, your clients need to arrive no later than noon or 1 p.m. if they sail at 5 p.m. or later. And post-cruise, you would not want to schedule a flight prior to noon, with the exception of Fort Lauderdale (where I would make sure it's not prior to 11 a.m.).

Recently, many cruise lines have decided to get back in the air ticket game, and have given agents the tools to book air through their online portals. The benefit of this to you is that it is sometimes commissionable, as well as covered under the cruise line's insurance policy. It also puts the responsibility of the cruise line to get your client to the cruise in a timely manner, and if there is a problem, the cruise line will have to handle it. (Although I would always tell my client to call me if there was any problem getting to the ship, so I could be sure they were taken care of expeditiously.)

The cruise lines do *so* many air tickets that the airlines are happy to give them contracts with reduced air fare from most major cities, especially Los Angeles, Chicago, Dallas, New York, and most major airline hubs. Just imagine embarkation day in Fort Lauderdale when the *Oasis* or *Allure of the Seas*, plus all the other ships are "turning around"! That's more than 5,000 air tickets into FLL just for that one RCCL ship, let alone all the others!

Eighty-five percent of your clients will have to fly to their cruise, so I always follow this protocol:

1. Do they have air miles, and want to do their own air? (I love this because, frankly, I don't really like doing air!)

2. Do they have a preferred air carrier, and are they a member of any frequent flyer air programs? If so, I would try to use those carriers, but still price all airlines so I can give them a choice.

3. Check with the cruise line air program to see what they offer. They sometimes have restricted air tickets and non-restrictedair tickets.

   Restricted air ticket means that there are restrictions on changes and cancellations; usually there are no cancellations or changes without a fee, up to 100% of the value of the ticket. These are the least expensive tickets, and are sometimes much less than the price you or the passenger could find themselves due to air contracts the cruise line has with the airline.

   Unrestricted air ticket means changes or cancellations are allowed, sometimes for a small fee (e.g., $50). It is important that you check the fare rules that come with the ticket so you can inform your passenger accordingly. These tickets can sometimes be as expensive as first-class tickets, depending on the fare code used. If your passenger needs the flexibility of changing dates, names, etc., then this may be the fare to opt for.

4. An important thing to consider is if your passenger needs extra room due to height, weight, preference, or medical necessity. A few of the airlines have options, such as Economy Plus with United Airlines, or American Airlines' extra legroom seats, where the passenger pays a fee over and above the restricted airfare to get six inches more legroom towards the front of the aircraft. This is totally worth the extra $39 to $139, especially if your passenger is very tall, or needs more room for any reason. Each airline has their own procedure on booking these seats, so make sure you familiarize yourself with these programs on

the individual airline's websites. If the extra legroom is desired, then it may behoove you to book the air for them rather than using the cruise line's air program, so you can be sure to hand-pick the seats and class of service. You may not make any commission on the ticket, but for me, it's worth it for my client to arrive and depart their cruise in comfort, otherwise it may taint their cruise experience. I make money off the cruise commission, so that satisfies me.

5. Air Deviation Fee: If you client wants to leave early and make their own hotel arrangements, or stay past disembarkation day, plus you want to book your air tickets through the cruise line, you may have to pay an Air Deviation Fee. This enables you to choose your outbound and homebound dates and flights. Some cruise lines allow you to do everything via their travel agent portal (e.g., POLAR has EZ Air). Otherwise, you will have to call or fax in your air deviation request, and the air department of the cruise line will get back to you with flights. I have always found it best to choose the flights I want for my client, and then see if the cruise line can arrange those within the cost parameter of the Air Deviation Fee and airfare charged by the cruise line. The benefits of doing air through the cruise line are that they are responsible for your client if anything goes wrong with those flights. They are also covered by the cruise line insurance if your client takes their policy. Air Deviation Fees (not including upgrades or fare differences) usually run between $50 to $150 per person.

You can consider charging an air research or ticketing fee if you end up doing the research and booking the tickets for your client; a typical fee would be $25 to $50 per ticket. This is even if you use a consumer online website or book it for them via telephone. Your time *is* worth money, so I would look at how much you are making in cruise commission. If it is a big ticket cruise with a lot of commission, I might consider waiving this, but if you are doing air for a shorter cruise with less than $200 commission, then I would definitely consider charging the air research fee.

I use my own private labeled website through my host agency to research air; my agency has contracts with some of the major airlines, so sometimes our fares are far less than either the cruise line's or consumer website's, even with the $50 per ticket fee my host agency charges to do air tickets. This pulls up all of the different air schedule possibilities for me so I can make informed suggestions for my client. If you do not have a host agency or website, I also use www.kayak.com for researching purposes only. When it comes time to book, I always use the actual airline's website (not Travelocity or Expedia, etc.) The reason I only use the actual website for the airline is because if you need to make any changes to that reservation, including on the day of departure at the airport, your client would have to go to the alternative website to do so; they cannot upgrade, change flights, or anything without going through the portal they booked! I once made a booking through Expedia on American Airlines, and when I got to the airport, I would have been able to upgrade to first class with my miles – but because I did not book directly with the airline, they would not allow me to, even though the entire cabin in first class was wide open and I had plenty of miles! If a flight is cancelled and your client needs to go on another flight to get to their cruise, they would have to call the other portal to re-book and use their existing ticket (often impossible). If you book through the airline's website, they are able to change right there at the airport, giving your client much more flexibility and ability to problem-solve their situation by themselves.

Hotels

Most cruise lines offer hotel packages in conjunction with their cruises, both pre- and post-cruise. What is the benefit of booking a hotel through the cruise line? The most important benefit is convenience to your client. The hotel package usually includes pickup from the airport to the hotel, porterage, room accommodation, sometimes breakfast, then transportation from the hotel to the ship. (The same is true in reverse for post-cruise hotel packages.) Some cruise lines have extended hotel stays that also include sightseeing tours. It is important you check with each individual cruise line to make sure if it includes any transfers, tours or meals; don't assume breakfast is included unless it is specifically stated. The packages tend to run significantly more than just booking the hotel directly, but there are many components to consider, including the expense of transfers and baggage handling. If your travelers are fairly inexperienced, these packages are a great way for them to see a pre- and post-cruise city with a fair amount of handholding. If they are experienced, then it may be to their benefit to book directly with the hotel. I will sometimes find out the name of the hotel the cruise line is using, and try to book it directly with the hotel chain. If the savings is negligible, then I book through the cruise line. If it is $100 or more savings, then it may be worth booking directly, but make sure you look into how much it would cost for transfers both from the airport to the hotel and then the hotel to the ship. It cities like Rome, the airport is forty-five minutes to an hour away from the city center, and the ship is well over an hour from city center to the port, so the hotel package makes sense, even for experienced travelers. The cruise lines annually research the best hotels for their passengers, so you can be assured they are getting a beautiful property, and your clients will be happy.

A rule of thumb for me is if a passenger cannot fly to an embarkation port prior to noon, then I strongly recommend they take a hotel package, or at least arrive the day before and get a hotel on their own. After two decades in the cruise industry, I have seen too many passengers miss ships due to airline delays. Even for Caribbean cruises, if a passenger is from the West Coast, I practically insist they arrive the day prior, just to be sure. Booking through the cruise line just makes everything that much easier for them. Plus, you get commission through the cruise line! (I'm still awaiting commissions due to me from some Rome hotels that were booked directly more than two years ago!)

Insurance

As far as I'm concerned, insurance is a must. I try to never sell a cruise without also selling insurance to go with it. I have dozens and dozens of horror stories about passengers who refused insurance, swore they never needed it, and had catastrophic things happen to them. I have my own stories as well, and thank God we had insurance! My father passed away on a ship, and can you imagine what we would have had to pay to get him home from Costa Rica had we not had insurance? One of the first cruises I sold as a new cruise agency was to a family of six; their twelve-year-old daughter had her appendix burst in the middle of the Mexican Riviera, and they had to airlift her by helicopter off the ship and fly her to San Diego. She would have died had they not had the resources to evacuate her as expeditiously they did, and they would have not had those resources without travel insurance!

Cruise lines have cancellation penalties based on the amount of time prior to sailing that you make your cancellation. Usually within a week of sailing, it is 100% cancellation penalty, and woe is the traveler who does not take insurance! I had a client who bought a $100,000 world cruise and insisted on not taking insurance because they were going no matter what. The husband passed away a week prior to sailing, and the cruise line categorically refused to refund even a penny of their cruise fare, no matter how much she begged, pleaded, and threatened to sue. The cancellation penalties are very clearly delineated in the cruise contract, and their lawyers have made sure that contract is ironclad. In the old days, the cruise lines were more flexible and understanding about refunding in cases such as death, but not anymore. They cannot afford to make *any* exceptions, because then everyone would want the cruise line to make an exception for their situation.

Most cruise lines have fairly good insurance policies that they sell in conjunction with their cruises. There are a number of other great companies that sell travel insurance separately, including Travelex and Travel Guard, my two favorites. The benefit of selling insurance through the cruise line is they often have a benefit that if you cancel for an uninsured reason (not medical, death, or other covered reason as specified in their brochure), you can keep a portion of your cruise fare as a future cruise credit, and not lose it completely.

The other travel companies (like Travelex) have very specific reasons one is covered for, so if a passenger needs to cancel for something other than what is listed, they may lose the penalty amount of their cruise fare. I am very specific about this in the correspondence I send my clients, because I do not want *any* discrepancy about refunds if they need to cancel. You do not want your client to say that you never told them about the penalties, or blame you for not explaining the necessity of cancellation insurance. I make them sign a Reservation Authorization (Appendix, page 146) that has them initial if they accept or decline insurance from either the cruise line or an alternative insurance company. I also enclose information about cancellation penalties in my Limiting Terms and Conditions (Appendix, page 138), so they have it in writing.

I personally will compare my insurance company of choice with the cruise line's policy and let the client know the price of both. If it is a family, sometimes the independent insurance company will cover children younger than eighteen or twenty-one for free, so there can be a significant savings for the client. This is all part of good customer service, and you can be sure if they need to use the policy, they will thank you for it!

Gratuities

Gratuities (or tips) are a very important part of the cost of a cruise, so it is vital you discuss these with your cruise passengers, especially those who have never cruised before.

Some cruise lines will have you pre-pay gratuities with the cruise fare. This is typically done with large groups. (You can sometimes negotiate pre-paid gratuities as a benefit to your group through consortiums, such as Virtuoso.)

Carnival Cruise Lines prefers it if you pre-pay gratuities, especially for the shorter three- or four-day cruises, or holiday cruises. (A rep for Carnival shared with me that many passengers on three-day holiday sailings remain inebriated the entire time, forgetting to pay their gratuities upon departure of the ship!) Your client can choose to add the gratuities onto their total cruise bill prior to departure so they don't have to worry about them once they get onboard the ship.

You may be wondering, why all this fuss about gratuities? Gratuities are a very important part of the cruise business, especially for waiters, assistant waiters, room stewards, and bar staff – they are often *not paid* **any salary**, and have to work exclusively for gratuities! How do the cruise lines get away with this? They have done so since I have been working in the business; I think the British room stewards on Princess and Cunard were paid a salary when I first started, but once the cruise lines started to merge with each other (Princess with Sitmar in 1988, etc.), the pay scale for these positions kept disappearing until they became gratuities-only. (I remember several British room stewards on Princess who had houses in England *and* the south of France because they made such good money onboard the ships! They all quit after the merger because the cruise line was able to bring in other nationalities who would work for no salary.) This is why you will not see any Americans working in these positions (on any ships other than the *Pride of America*/Norwegian Cruise Lines); our labor laws forbid what amounts to slave labor, so you will typically find nationalities from less advantaged countries. These employees work sixteen+ hour days with hardly any break, and no days off! *They earn their tips*!

The cruise line counts on about $13.00 to $23.50 per person, per day (the current rate in the industry) in gratuities for these staff members. If a family chooses to *not* tip their room steward or wait-staff in the dining room, it is a significant pay cut for those employees, and the cruise line will not make it up to them. This is quite devastating when it happens, because often they send their entire collection of tips back home to support all of their family members, keeping very little for themselves.

For an interesting look at the life of a waiter onboard Carnival Cruise ships, check out Brian David Brun's book, *Cruise Confidential: A Hit Below the Waterline.* It's a true account of his year as a waiter on board the *Carnival Conquest.* He fell in love with a Romanian woman who worked on board the ships, and convinced Carnival to hire him so he could be with her. He is the only American to survive training and actually work for a period of time as a crew member onboard a Carnival ship! You won't believe the long hours, grueling work, emotional toil, and very little compensation these employees endure, but Brian shares it all in this book in an amusing, entertaining, and informative way. I have such a deep appreciation for these crew members now! The book will help you to understand the importance of gratuities, and also explain them to your clients prior to their departure.

Bar staff are typically tipped out at 15% of the total bar bill. The gratuity is automatically added on when drinks are ordered. In the 1970s and 1980s, passengers would write in a tip amount, but now it is just added on. You can choose to take the gratuity off the bill, or even add more on if you feel the person earned it. Then, at the end of the cruise, the computers add up all the gratuities that individual staff member earned, and it is deposited in their shipboard account. (The ship acts like a huge bank for all the crew members; they can then withdraw their tips to send home via Western Union.)

For your room steward, waiter, assistant waiter, and head waiter, a cumulative gratuity is charged to your shipboard account on a daily basis. You need to tell your cruise passengers that this is going to occur. The amount, as discussed above, is currently around $13.50-$23.50 *per person, per day.* (Yes, even for little children.) You can choose to take this gratuity off of your shipboard account and pay the tips directly to the staff. Personally, I think it makes everything easier having them charged to my account, but there is always a fear that the tips will not get to those who deserve them most. Because I feel they work so hard, I usually give my room steward and waiter an extra $20, and assistant waiter an extra $10 on the first day of the cruise, telling them "Thank you in advance for everything you are going to do for me and my family this week." This ensures I get the very best effort from them, because they know I'm going to tip them at the end of the cruise as well, plus they are so appreciative that someone thought of them in advance. (The exception to this is if I have Personal Choice or My Time dining, when there is a different waiter every night).

There are several Luxury cruise lines (Crystal, Regent, and Silversea, to name a few) that are all-inclusive. This includes not only all of your beverages (even wine, beer, bottled water, soft drinks and hard liquor), but also gratuities as well. Some even include basic shore excursions in each port. The crew members are paid a good salary, and are told to politely refuse tips when offered. The cruise fare is substantially higher with these cruise lines, but you definitely get what you pay for! The service is wonderful, and it is refreshing to not be nickled-and-dimed everywhere you turn.

If you are booking a Luxury cruise, make sure to check if gratuities are included so you can inform your clients accordingly. These additional charges are very important considerations, as they do add up, especially for large families. I have sometimes done price comparisons between a Luxury all-inclusive cruise line and a Mass Market cruise line, and have found once you add in gratuities, shore excursions, and drinks, the Luxury cruise line is sometimes less expensive than the Mass Market cruise line! (Especially if the clients are big drinkers.)

FIT VS GROUPS

What is FIT, and what is a group? That was the essential question we all had when we first started at Princess Cruises in August 1984. We had heard the two terms bandied about in practically every conversation about cruise bookings and travel. The terms are basically the same as they were in 1984, but the importance of where you, as a travel agent today, place your bookings has changed throughout the years.

FIT means Free Independent Travel. The term describes a traveler who is not booked in a group. It also tends to describe someone paying full fare for a trip, often with several components of an itinerary – i.e., air ticket, hotel, possibly cruise – but reserving each component separately.

Group means the person is booked in a block of rooms, or staterooms, or air tickets, etc., and possibly each of the components is combined together to give a total price that is often less expensive than booking each component separately.

For cruises, a group means that the agency is holding a block of staterooms on a given ship and sailing date, giving the agency benefits and sometimes a lower price. Over the years, cruise lines have gone back and forth about offering a lower price to groups. At one point, a major cruise line said that they would not offer a lower price because they wanted to give every travel agent the same price across the board, regardless of whether or not they had a large group of people or just one stateroom booked. The pendulum has come back to the other side, and most cruise lines will offer either a lower cruise fare (usually around $50), or amenity or Group Amenity Point (GAP) if the agency books a group.

Amenity or GAP Points

Amenity points are offered as an incentive to agencies to book groups. They range from 1 point all the way up to 10 points (or higher) depending on the destination, length of sailing, and need for the cruise line to entice groups on a particular itinerary. What are these points for? They can be used to "buy" gifts, upgrades, or even a bonus commission for the agency. Typically they are used for bottles of wine, photographs, chocolate-covered strawberries, and alternative dining. They can also be used for onboard credits for your clients, from $10 per stateroom all the way up to $100. These onboard credits can be used for their bar tab, soft drinks, shore excursions, in the gift shop...anywhere onboard they can charge on their cruise card, with the exception of the casino. I like giving the onboard credits because the message on the gift card says it's from me, and the perceived value is that I gave them money back for their cruise, when it doesn't cost me a thing!

Now, here is something very important for you to know (that the cruise lines don't necessarily want you to know!): I will *always* try to book a group around every one of my cruise bookings! The cruise lines are wonderful about honoring the group amenities even though you might not have reached the number of staterooms needed for their minimum (typically eight staterooms). Some cruise lines are better about this than others; Princess is wonderful about their groups and always honors the amenities if I have assigned where I want the points to go. RCCL and Celebrity are a bit harder to work with because their group reservation computer system is different than their individual reservation computer system, so you have to deal exclusively with their group department once you have a group on a sailing. With Princess, Cunard, and Holland America (all on POLAR), once you have a group on a sailing, any bookings you make *will automatically slide right into your group!* (With the exception of FLASH FARE bookings – they are exempt from groups.) For RCCL, Celebrity, and Azamara (Cruising Power), plus Carnival

Cruise Lines, you have to actually put your bookings in the group; they won't automatically be put into them unless you go into the group side of their computer system. With Carnival, you have a choice at the time of booking of which fare you want to use, so at that point you can designate it as a group booking. I know it may seem a little confusing, but once you are in the system, it will make sense. If I have two staterooms or more that I am booking on a sailing, I always set up a group for it so I can get the amenity (or GAP) points and hopefully lower fares.

Your main reservation systems online are POLAR (again, for Princess, Cunard, and Holland America) and Cruising Power (for RCCL, Celebrity, and Azamara). There is also Book CCL for Carnival Cruise Lines and Norwegian Central for NCL. Please take some time and take their tutorials now on how to book cruises online. This will save you so much time because you will be able to make bookings in the middle of the night, weekends, holidays…any time that the reservation office is closed, you have access to all of their inventory, as if you are working at the cruise line itself! These systems have revolutionized how travel agents can sell cruises, and it is worth every minute you spend to learn these systems. I started with POLAR because I was selling so much Princess (due to my former employment there) and it was a very easy system to learn…. I suggest you start there. Right now. Put this book down and go to the computer and take the POLAR tutorial! https://book.princess.com

Tour Conductors – or "Cruise for Free!"

What is a Tour Conductor (or TC, as it's fondly known as)? You have probably seen the enticement to "cruise for free – ask me how!" The "cruise for free" refers to a TC. Most cruise lines have a TC policy; the most common number of staterooms needed to earn a TC is eight staterooms, or sixteen lower berths. If you have this minimum booked *in a group*, you get a "free" berth. The staterooms have to be booked in an official group; you cannot have eight *separate* staterooms on the same sailing from the same agency and get the TC. I have had that happen! I had eight staterooms booked on a seven-day coastal cruise from Los Angeles; they did not know each other, and I did not have the foresight to create a group through the cruise line. I did not even realize I had eight bookings until I started to do their onboard gifts and saw just how many were going on the same ship and sailing date! When I approached the cruise line for a TC, they denied me because the bookings were not part of an official group. I could have had amenity points, a TC for me, and possibly lower fares had I just created a group when I booked the first two cabins.

So now, I always create a group around my bookings, just in case. Worst-case scenario is I don't get the amenity points (which my clients did not know about anyway), and they are just relegated back to general reservations because I did not make the minimum needed to sustain the group. Because I'm part of a host agency, there are hundreds of travel agents booking into the groups, so there may be a possibility that between us, we come up with eight staterooms. This happened last week; I received a call from my host agency saying we had earned a TC on a group that I had started by booking two staterooms. (Because they were not all my bookings, we took the value of the TC and split it as extra commission between the agents who booked their clients on this sailing. Hey, a little extra commission is nice now and then!)

I offer the TC to anyone who can put together a group of at least eight staterooms for me. I'm sure you know someone who can be a pied piper for your business...the kind of person who knows everyone, and loves to organize people? This is what the TC was designed for – to reward the person who refers groups of people to you and the cruise line. Use this wonderful amenity to build groups for your business.

MONEY MATTERS

Deposits

If you are booking a cruise more than sixty to seventy-five days prior to sailing, you will be asked to make an initial deposit to hold the booking. Once you are within sixty to seventy-five days prior to sailing, the full payment will be required. (Sometimes, World Cruises or very expensive cruises will require a second deposit as well, but this will be clearly explained at the time of booking.)

Deposits vary from cruise line to cruise line. Sometimes it is a percentage of the total cruise fare; other times it is a set dollar amount. Often, if the cruise line is running a special promotional fare, they will require an immediate, non-refundable deposit at the time of booking. If this is the case, the client will need a credit card to hold the booking.

Deposits can be made with a check or a credit card. If it is a check, the client will make it out to the agency, and the agency will send a check or Electronic Payment (if they are set up for this) to the cruise line. The easiest by far, however, is by credit card. I strongly encourage clients to make all payments by credit card, for several reasons. First of all, it protects them; the credit card is processed directly by the cruise line, so there is no middleman (i.e., the travel agent) dealing with the actual money. I cannot tell you how many times I have heard of unscrupulous travel agents taking cash and check payments for deposits and disappearing with them. If anything goes awry with a deposit or final payment (i.e., payment was made, but not to the cruise line but to the travel agent's personal account), the client has recourse through the credit card company to reverse the charges. Many credit card companies have additional insurance (Accidental Death and Dismemberment, etc.) if they make travel payments with their card.

For me as their agent, using a credit card makes things much easier than having to deal with making payments by check to the cruise line. If clients want to pay cash or with a check, they have to pay at least two weeks prior to the due date so I can ensure the check clears, have time to issue an agency check, pay for the expense of mailing said check (via a trackable mailing system such as Fed Ex or Priority Mail), and give everything time to be posted and cleared. With a credit card, I can either post payment via the cruise line's website, or call it in and have it applied immediately.

It is important to note that prices are not guaranteed until a deposit is posted. Make sure to also note the cruise line's refund policy on deposits; usually the deposit is fully refundable to the client up until final payment. Once final payment is due, cancellation penalties begin. (Although Royal Caribbean has instituted a no-refund policy on their deposits.)

Many cruise lines will now cancel your booking and refund the deposit if final payment is not made by the final payment due date! It is *very important* that you do not let this happen, because the price may have gone up between the time you booked it and the time final payment is due, so if your booking cancels, very often you cannot get the same price you had before! I usually tell my client final payment is due five to seven days prior to when the cruise line requires it so this does not happen.

Another scenario you want to avoid is trying to cancel the day after final payment is due and penalties start to accrue, because very often you will be charged the full deposit amount even if final payment has not been made. Once, very early in my career, a client called at 6 p.m. on a Saturday to cancel the day before final payment was due; things came up and I did not get around to canceling the reservation until Monday, and the cruise line assessed the deposit amount as penalty! (I was able to reverse it, but it took a lot of begging and pulling of strings.) Now that everything is online, you can access your bookings twenty-four hours a day, seven days a week, so you should be able to apply payments and cancel reservations in a timely manner. Chances are the cruise line would not have reversed my error if I had made it now, due to this accessibility online – I would have had no excuse!

FINAL PAYMENT

As mentioned above, I tell my clients that final payment is due five to seven days prior to the due date the cruise line gives me. This avoids cancellation by the cruise line if payment is not received in their office by that day. I have a calendar in the top drawer of my desk in which I record every deposit and final payment, and I check it each and every morning to see what needs to be done *first* that day. I also record when to do gift orders and send out documents to my clients (more on those later). I highly recommend having some sort of system for this, whether you put these dates in your phone, your online calendar, or a paper calendar that is used exclusively for your daily tasks for your business.

Many people will ask about payment plans; they cannot afford to do two big payments (deposit and final), but want to pay something on a monthly basis. This is very easily done with a credit card. I have a client who is going on a world cruise in two years, and wants to put several thousand dollars a month towards his balance, so on the 10th of every month I process his credit card online (on his booking in POLAR), send him an updated invoice, and he is all set!

What if they want to pay with cash or check? You can do that as well, but as a travel agent, in several states you are required to establish a trust (similar to an escrow) account to hold these funds. If you are with an established host agency, they will typically have this account set up for you, but if you are opening up your own agency, check with the requirements in your state. Several states (such as Washington and California) also require you to post a surety or bond, so make sure you have checked that out. (I will not go into all the different requirements per state in this book, as they periodically change, but it is vital that these are scrupulously paid attention to so you are not shut down just as you are getting started! The easiest way to handle this is to join a well-established host agency. That's how I handled all of the State of California requirements.). You can then send the payments as you receive them via agency check to the cruise line, or keep them in the escrow account until final payment is due. Remember to allow enough time for a check to post and clear with a cruise line, typically two weeks prior to due date. Many cruise lines will not allow the travel agent to use their own personal or agency credit card to make payments; i.e., the client pays the agency, and the agency pays the cruise line with a credit card. I know it seems like it would make things much easier, but they must have had some big problems with charge-backs, so they have made a rule disallowing agency credit cards. Again, check with the cruise line if you were thinking of doing this with your cash and check-paying clients.

FARE CHECKING

Do you want to be an excellent travel agent and have clients come back to you again and again? Do you want them to refer you to all of their friends who are thinking about cruising? The secret is quite easy…be their advocate and give excellent customer service. How do you do that? Fare-checking.

I can usually lower the fare of my clients in about 70% of my bookings. I set aside one day per month where I go booking by booking and pull up the sailing they are on to check and see if the price has gone down. If it has, I either re-fare it in the computer, or I call reservations and ask them to "protect" the lower fare for me. Does it lower my commissions? Yes, and sometimes the reduction is substantial. But, it is totally worth it! Can you imagine your client sitting up on deck at the Lido café, talking to someone who booked 4 months after your client did, and their fare was hundreds of dollars less than what they paid? It happens all the time, where passengers talk with one another about how much they paid; if I have lowered their fare, they are usually bragging about what a great travel agent they have in me, and giving away all the extra business cards I have given them as referral cards. A full 100% of my business has grown exclusively from referrals; I do *no* advertising at all, because I am so busy with all of the referrals I have been blessed with! I attribute it completely to my excellent customer service because of my fare-checking.

Fares go down all the time; different promotions are introduced, past-passenger discounts come up, and the cruise lines are usually very good about protecting the lower fare. The only fares that are definitely *not* protected are when the cruise line comes out with a "Flash Fare." These are typically within six to eight weeks of sailing, and happen when the cruise lines have a lot of extra space on your sailing that they need to fill. These staterooms are usually in the very front, very back, or at the bottom of the ship. If you find a flash fare and, for example, you see that a balcony is less than what your clients paid for an ocean view or interior stateroom, the cruise lines may not be able to "protect" the lower fare, but they may be able to do something for your clients; e.g., upgrade them to the balcony for the price they are originally paying – or I've even seen cruise lines give onboard credits to help offset the difference.

It is important that when you call the cruise line to discuss the situation, especially with flash fares, you are very nice to the reservation agent. They get yelled at all day by travel agents who are angry that the cruise line came out with these flash fares (which can make the travel agent look like he/she is charging too much). It's not the reservation agent's fault that the cruise line has a flash fare, but they do have the power to help you, if you are willing to work with them. Every cruise line is different, and every flash fare is different, so if you see a flash fare, call reservations, be nice, and ask if there is anything they can do for you. They cannot bring the fare lower, but if they like you, they will often go to bat for you with a supervisor and try to do something. If your clients are the ones who find the lower fare, you can tell them that because they booked so far in advance they have the best staterooms on the ship...the flash fare staterooms are the leftovers and not staterooms your clients would be happy with if location is important to them. But, if you call and try, you may be able to offer your client some concessions, depending on what the cruise line can do for you.

When you are checking for the lower fares, it is important that you use your client's past-passenger number (if they are a past passenger) in the computer to pull up the new fares. Why? Some past passengers are offered specials that other past passengers or first timers are not offered, so it's important that you use the number to get the very lowest price that is applicable to your client. If you have several staterooms, and some passengers are offered a lower price than others, then you can call the cruise line to see how you can get the same price for everyone that is sailing. They can do a "share the fare" or something similar, if it is available.

Documents

DEPOSIT PACKETS

When clients book a cruise, they are investing a lot of money in a vacation. I feel it is important that I acknowledge this with a deposit packet of information. I want them to be able to hold in their hands proof that they are going somewhere spectacular. With that in mind, I have created a detailed deposit packet for my clients. Following are the components of this deposit packet. (Note: examples of all of this paperwork can be found in the Appendix on page 137.)

A folder to hold everything in place

Left side:

- A self-addressed, stamped envelope to send back to me
- Reservation Authorization (to sign and send back to me)
- My Limiting Terms and Conditions
- A copy of the Reservation Authorization for their files
- Insurance information depending on the insurance they have chosen

Right side:

- Letter of congratulations
- Invoice from the Cruise Line
- Any other pertinent information; i.e., visa application, hotel information, etc.
- Information on needing a passport and cruise line sign-on information

Reservation Authorization

The Reservation Authorization is perhaps the most important document you will ever use in your business. It protects you and your business from litigation against you in the event of the cruise line's negligence. It has several components:

1. An introduction, asking them to return the form to you
2. The details of their cruise, including the proper spelling of their names, ship, sailing date, etc.
3. Booking number
4. First statement that any changes will result in penalties
5. Statement that rates and fares not guaranteed until paid in full
6. Insurance Advisory – They need to initial whether they accept or decline insurance. You *need* this *in writing* because if something happens during the penalty period, it's your word against theirs.
7. Payment Authorization – Credit card information. I do not put the entire credit card number, just the first four numbers and last two, so they know which card they used. This is a credit card receipt that corresponds to the invoice that is included in the packet.
8. Signature agreement statements – These are especially important because they protect you by saying the client read the Limiting Terms and Conditions.
9. Signature

I say that final documents cannot be released until this form is signed and returned. Now that they can print their documents from the Internet, this is hard to enforce, but it gives it a sense of urgency, and I have never had a problem collecting this form.

Limiting Terms and Conditions

The Limiting Terms and Conditions are *very, very important* to your business. Take a few minutes and go to page 138 and read them. You will see that this covers everything! I've even included a paragraph relieving me of responsibility if I've gone online and accepted the cruise line's passage of contract on their behalf. This is because I am often the first person to log on to their booking on the cruise line's website, and the website requires you accept the cruise line's contract at that point.

The paperwork talks about the need for a passport, documentation, baggage, check-in, reconfirmation, tickets, change of plans, the importance of insurance, cancellations, itineraries (I'll explain why this is important below), special needs, traveling by air, air deviation, payments, and taxes/surcharges (such as fuel supplements). I wouldn't have thought itineraries would have been that big of a deal, but I will share with you why it is so important.

Truthfully, this is still a hard story for me to share, but I think it's important for you to hear because you never would have believed it from a friend. I had a friend who booked a cruise to the Eastern Caribbean more than fifteen months prior to sailing. The cruise line was a fairly new one, with just three ships, and didn't even have brochures out at that point for the time period the cruise was sailing. Their confirmations at the time did not specify either Western or Eastern Caribbean, just Caribbean (this was a very long time ago...this has since changed). When the brochures came out, there was no notice of an itinerary change to the Western Caribbean, and there was really no way for me to know without looking at the brochure of a cruise that had been booked several months prior. When the documents came, the shore excursion booklet was for both the Eastern and Western Caribbean, and the cruise ticket just specified Caribbean. My friend got to the ship, went to book her shore excursions for Eastern, and was told the itinerary was now Western Caribbean. She was absolutely furious; however, she booked excursions, and went on to enjoy the cruise. When she came home, she sued me and the agency for not delivering the itinerary she was promised. Even though she went on the cruise and enjoyed herself, she claimed it was not the cruise she paid for!

The cruise line even offered to give her a *free* cruise to the Eastern Caribbean, but she would have to pay for her airfare to get there. She refused (her traveling companion was her grandmother, and she said Grandma was too old and tired to go on another cruise) and persisted with her lawsuit. We had to pay her back for her cruise out of pocket, and hope that E&O Insurance would cover it. Needless to say, she is no longer a friend, and I will never make that mistake ever again! I double and triple check itineraries, and also now have my Reservation Authorization absolving me from any itinerary changes for any reason. So hopefully you will learn from my mistake! That was the one and only problem I've had with a passenger and itineraries.

Invoice

The invoice is also a very important document. It states all the pertinent information about the ship, cruise line, and sailing date, and then goes into detail about what is due and when. Most of the time I will use the invoice from the cruise line showing that the deposit has been made. Make sure you enclose the Passenger Copy of the invoice and not the Agency Copy.

I also include instructions on how to log on to the cruise line's website and complete their mandatory immigration and emergency contact information. Every passenger must do this in order to sail, so I put it front and center for them to see. I ask them to advise me once they have completed this process so I may print out their documents and baggage tags.

CRUISE DOCUMENTS

Years ago, cruise lines would spend millions of dollars sending out beautiful ticket packets, complete with cruise tickets, air tickets (if booked through the cruise line), cruise answer booklets, shore excursion brochures, baggage tags, and any other information the cruise line needed to impart to their passengers. With the advent of e-tickets for airlines, cruise lines got smart, seeing a way to save literally millions of dollars in postage and printing by making all of that information available on the web. It's taken awhile for this to catch on, but now passengers, for the most part, are able to access everything they need online, typically seventy-five days prior to sailing. The big exceptions to this would be the older passengers who are not Internet savvy and don't know how to access cruise line websites. However, just because someone is in their seventies or eighties, do not make the assumption they are not online! Many of my older clients have nothing better to do but be online for hours at a time, researching lower fares, port guides, etc. I always check with each client to see how comfortable they are with the Internet. If they are not, then I walk them through the whole process while I am online and they are either in front of me or on the phone.

In the past, the cruise lines had passengers fill out a Passenger Information Form (or PIF) at the ship on the day of embarkation. Since September 11th, 2001, cruise lines are now required to collect all of this information at least two weeks prior to embarkation because their lists are then sent to the FBI for review. A couple of months ago, I read about a man who was arrested at the ship at embarkation; the FBI had been looking for him for several years for serious tax evasion, and they were able to catch up with him because he filled out all of his pertinent information for the cruise line! I've heard horror stories of people being arrested at disembarkation after they have cruised because of this as well, so be aware that these lists *are* taken seriously by the FBI, and they are checked over with a fine-tooth comb.

What kind of information is collected? The basics, such as name, address, phone number, etc. Then they collect passport number, date of issue, place of issue, expiration date, and emergency contact information. They also require a credit card number that will be used for onboard purchases once the passenger is on the ship. This credit card number can be changed once they get there, or they can also pay cash once they are onboard, but most require a credit card number in order to complete the online registration.

Once this online registration is complete, the passenger can then print their boarding pass and any documents the cruise line feels they need. Personally, I make sure this is done at least a month prior to sailing. I check each and every client because this is when we often find out that a passport might be expired, or they have misplaced it somewhere, and it still gives us a little bit of time to solve whatever problem may come up because of it.

I also send my clients some gifts prior to sailing; I found a vendor who put my logo on some inexpensive tote bags. So, I will print their boarding passes, any documentation on embarkation, insurance information (if they've purchased through the cruise line), and any other paperwork I feel they may need, along with tote bags and baggage tags. I know they can print their boarding passes themselves, but it just adds that little bit of customer service that online agencies don't give them; it sets me apart, and they remember these little things. You can tell your clients to just print what they need, but anticipation is half the fun, so when they receive my packet in the mail, it brings them that much closer to their dream cruise vacation.

A note about baggage tags. The cruise lines now have the passengers print these lame baggage tags that they are supposed to staple or tape around the handles of their suitcases. I found a vendor that makes plastic bag tag holders that look very professional, and make me look like I know what I'm doing! I just slide the cruise line's bag tags into the plastic bag tag holders, put my business card on the back side, and viola! Beautiful bag tags for my clients! If you are just starting out, you don't necessarily need to spend the money on bag tags or tote bags, but as you grow, these are two good investments in your business. It keeps your name out there and where your client is likely to look when it's time to rebook. (Please see the index for the vendor's name if you are interested.)

GIFT ORDERS

Gift orders are completely up to you. These are gifts that are delivered to your client's stateroom, either at embarkation or sometime during the course of their cruise. It is a very personal decision whether to send something to your clients. In the "old days," a travel agent would typically send a bottle of wine with a note, because that was all the cruise line offered. Now, cruise lines have brochures dedicated to all the different things they offer. You can get anything from bottles of wine, to gift certificates to the ship's signature restaurants (that charge a cover fee), to items from the gift shop (such as beach towels, sun visors, ship ornaments, cookbooks, the list goes on), to chocolate-dipped strawberries, to on-board credits. (The last two are two of my favorite gifts to give.)

It all depends on how much commission you are going to make. If it is a three-day cruise and I've made only $19 commission, I don't even send an onboard gift, and they get my tote bag prior to sailing. If it is a World Cruise and the commission is $8,000, you can bet I'm going to send *lots* of gifts! I usually send chocolate-dipped strawberries to be waiting in their stateroom at embarkation, and then something else, like an on-board credit or dinner at the signature restaurant. Princess Cruises has a balcony breakfast for two that is absolutely delightful, and very reasonable, so I will send that to my clients who are sailing in a balcony stateroom. It all depends on my commission and the cruise line.

I typically place my order a month prior to departure; this is close enough that I know they are sailing and won't cancel (unless there is a dire emergency), and far enough in advance that the cruise line will process my order with no problems. Every cruise line is different, so you will have to check with each cruise line to see how they handle their gift orders.

Remember, this is a token of your appreciation so it should not exceed 10% to 15% of your commission. You are in business to make money, so be wise in the amount you spend on gifts.

Deck Plans 101

YOU'VE MADE THE DECISION to sell cruises – now, how do you do it? What is a deck plan and how do you read one? Let's start at the very beginning (a very good place to start!)....

STATEROOMS AND BERTHS

There is a lot of confusion about the difference between a stateroom and a cabin. They are one and the same. I like to use *stateroom* just because it sounds nicer than cabin...a cabin reminds me of a house in the woods. A stateroom, on the other hand, is a room on a ship.

Inside the stateroom are berths, or beds. In the cruise world, beds are called berths, and assigning people to their cabins is called *berthing a stateroom.*

Most staterooms have two berths, or beds. In the early days of cruising, the berths were unmovable, and it was rare to find a ship where the berths were put together to make a queen-sized bed. I have many stories of grown men crying to me on embarkation day on Island or Pacific Princess because it was their honeymoon, and the berths were in an L-shaped configuration and unable to be moved together.

Nowadays berths are movable, and your client can decide whether they want twin beds or a queen-sized bed in their stateroom,. (The twin beds can be pushed together, and the steward puts a filler piece in the middle underneath the sheets).

If there are third and fourth berths, it is important to check if these are lower berths or upper berths. Lower berths are usually sofa beds or rollaways. Disney has Murphy beds in some of their staterooms. Upper berths are bunk beds. These are often narrower than regular beds, so you need to be aware of who is going to be sleeping in the bunk bed; if you have a family with Grandma or an older adult as the third or fourth person, an upper berth would be completely inappropriate for this family.

Royal Caribbean has some of their balcony staterooms designated as a four berths, but the third and fourth berths are actually one queen-sized sofa bed.

It is very important that you check on what the third and fourth berthing is composed of and make sure it is appropriate for the age and sexes of your clients. That sofa bed on RCCL would be inappropriate for two teenagers, Grandma and another child, or two adults. Calling the cruise line or even checking online will often answer your berthing questions.

There are many types of staterooms. Let's look at the basics:

Interior

This is a stateroom without a window, usually on the inside corridor of the ship. Interior staterooms are the least expensive rooms on the ship. Many cruise lines will put a mirror where a window would normally be, which gives the room more of an open feeling. Disney Cruise Line went so far as to put a virtual window on their newest ships, *The Disney Dream* and *Disney Fantasy*. They've hooked up cameras on the outside of the ship and these virtual windows show the view from these cameras, giving the illusion of having an ocean-view window. Royal Caribbean has virtual balconies on some of their ships! They are 80-inch HD screens complete with a railing and adjustable natural noises. These are found on the *Anthem, Quantum, Ovation, Navigator, Explorer, Voyager, Harmony* and *Symphony of the Seas.*

Promenade Staterooms

This is a category on Royal Caribbean Ships for their interior staterooms that have a picture window that overlooks their promenade shopping area. Technically they are interior as they do not have ocean views, but the window overlooking the promenade gives the illusion that there is an exterior view, albeit over their shopping area. These can sometimes be a little noisy if they are on the lower decks, but RCCL has done their best to make the glass windows as soundproof as possible. These rooms are a great value for those who need the less expensive stateroom, but feel claustrophobic in an interior room.

Royal Caribbean has also extended this idea out to "Boardwalk" and "Central Park" view staterooms on the *Oasis, Harmony, Symphony* and *Allure of the Seas*; these rooms are on the interior corridor of the ship, but have bay windows or sliding glass doors with balconies that overlook interior areas of the ship.

Ocean-View Staterooms

These are rooms with windows that overlook the ocean (as opposed to interior areas of the ship). They can sometimes have obstructions in front of the window; for example, a lifeboat or other architectural feature of the ship. These obstructions will sometimes obliterate the view from the window by 100%, so it is important when booking an obstructed view stateroom to find out the percentage of obstruction, and what the obstruction is. The obstructed view staterooms can be less expensive, and a good value for those who need to feel they have an outside stateroom, but cannot afford one. At least you get a feeling of sunlight coming through the window, even with an obstruction.

An ocean-view stateroom is sometimes referred to as an *outside* stateroom. It's important to do a price comparison of ocean-view staterooms with balcony staterooms, because sometimes a balcony room will be less than an ocean-view stateroom! Cruise lines are building ships with more and more balconies and fewer ocean-view rooms; thus, sometimes the ocean-view rooms sell out and the cruise line is left with a surplus of balcony staterooms, so they deep discount the balcony rooms and not the ocean-view room. For my money, I always try to up-sell the client to a balcony room. It's often only $50 or $100 difference between the two categories, and the client will be much happier with the balcony room.

Balcony Staterooms

The most plentiful of stateroom types, the balcony stateroom is just that...a room with a sliding glass door that opens up to a balcony. The balcony can either have an ocean view, or now some cruise lines are building rooms with balconies that overlook the interior of the ship (Royal Caribbean has led the way in this). Celebrity has a few categories on the Solstice Class Ships that have an obstruction in all of their balcony staterooms on certain decks, so make sure there is no obstruction when you book a balcony stateroom.

This stateroom type should always be where you start when you quote a cruise. Start high at the balcony rate, and then quote the lower categories. Clients are more likely to book a balcony when you start with this as their lead-in price.

Mini-Suites

Mini-suites are similar to balcony staterooms, but have more square footage and more amenities. It is important to do your due diligence and go online to see the different amenities and square footages, as each cruise line is different, and even each ship differs from other ships at the same cruise line.

Mini-suites are great for families, as they often have more room in the sitting area where the additional berths are located. The balconies are often much larger than in a regular balcony stateroom, and the bathrooms will often have a bathtub with a shower and more luxurious appointments. Again, each and every ship is different, so make sure to do your research on square footage, layout, and amenities.

Suites

These are the granddaddies of them all. Every suite can be different, and the amenities are as varied as you can imagine: how about a grand piano, full dining room table for eight, private Jacuzzis, private butlers, private bars, the list goes on.... On Royal Caribbean's *Oasis* class ships, there are so many different suites available, it will make your head spin! One suite sleeps fourteen comfortably and has *four* bedrooms! On Norwegian Cruise Lines, their Haven suites have a deck all to themselves, and a number of bedrooms and bathrooms that can be adjusted depending on how many people you are taking. It is vitally important you do your homework and research the amenities, square footage, and rules.

Often, the suites will show up as being wait-listed, and you just need to call the cruise line to request them. They don't like putting the biggest suites for sale to book on their travel agent portals because they want only serious inquiries. Otherwise, travel agents would book them and hold them on speculation without having a serious client in mind. So, if you have a client that wants one of the big suites, and it shows up as wait-listed, just call the cruise line to find out if it's available to book. There's nothing like the feeling you get when you sell one of those suites!

Family Staterooms

Some of the cruise lines have specific staterooms for families. The best example of this is Disney Cruise Line. They just *get* family cruising, and have built their ships with several different stateroom configurations that you won't find on any other cruise line.

The most important thing you need to consider is what the berthing is in the stateroom. Remember what I talked about above; make sure there are enough lower beds for those who need lower beds, and that the cruise line does not consider a sofa bed as two of those berths. I make it a point to verbally discuss the berthing with my client, and then put it in writing so it does not come back to bite me when they embark. There can be no surprises when that stateroom door opens!

Often, it is less expensive to book two connecting staterooms than a designated family room. A connecting stateroom will either have a door between two rooms (like connecting hotel rooms) or a door that closes off the two staterooms from the outside. The outside door creates a small hallway between the front doors of the staterooms, so a family can open their stateroom doors at night, but lock the outside door. If the connecting rooms have three or four berths each, you could have up to eight people with two bathrooms!

A family room might have a living room with a sofa bed and one to four bedrooms. Again, call the cruise line to ask the configuration, berthing, number of bathrooms, if there are upper berths, and what the cruise fare is for the third and fourth (and more if you need them) passengers. Like the suites, the cruise line will often not put the family staterooms for sale on the travel agent portal, and you will have to call in to the cruise line to book them.

CATEGORIES AND STATEROOM NUMBERS

The cruise lines use categories to designate the type and location of staterooms on a ship. Staterooms can be designated by letters, numbers, or a combination of both. It just depends on the cruise line. The stateroom number can often tell you if the stateroom is on the port or starboard side of the ship.

Port and Starboard

What are port and starboard? Port is the left side of the ship. An easy way to remember this is *port* has four letters in the name, similar to *left*. (That was the first thing I learned in my training class at Princess Cruises!). Starboard is the right side of the ship. Royal Caribbean has the second or third number in the stateroom number as either a 1, 2, or 3 for one side of the ship, and 5, 6, or 7 for the other, so stateroom 6554 would be on the port side of the *Monarch of the Seas*, and 6054 would be in the same location on the same deck (Deck 6) but on the starboard side of the ship. Princess has even numbers on the port side, and odd numbers on the starboard side. Don't worry, you aren't required to memorize each and every cruise line and their stateroom delineation, but it will start to come naturally as you book cruises and are working with deck plans.

The deck plan is your map to the ship. You can either find them at the back of the brochures that are sent out by the cruise line or you can download them online. When I first started, I downloaded (or cut out of brochures) all the deck plans for the cruise lines I thought I'd be selling the most and put them all in a binder that I keep on my desk; this way I have every deck plan at my fingertips and I don't have to go hunting around for a current brochure or website. I put each page in a plastic page protector to keep them from tearing. That binder has had years of use, and I highly recommend doing this. Also, if you are downloading and printing them, make sure your printer has color capabilities, because many of the categories are delineated by color.

ORDERING BROCHURES

Speaking about brochures, now would be a good time to order some! Every cruise line has different policies and procedures on how to order brochures, but you can usually do this by calling a toll-free number or going online. I would order only five of each to start with, because they take up a lot of room. I went to an office supply store and purchased a shelving unit that has 24 little cubbies that are the perfect size for brochures; it has 3 cubbies across and 8 down. I have it on top of my file cabinets, and the brochures are easily accessible for me whenever I need to include them in a deposit packet.

This first time, I would call in to order your brochures; this way you can ask for every type of brochure available at the time. Some cruise lines have World Atlas brochures that include every single voyage they are offering in a 1-year period. Some of these brochures will hopefully have deck plans in the back.

You can also get location specific brochures, especially Alaska, Europe, or the Caribbean. Alaska is the most popular summer destination (as well as Europe), so make sure you have plenty of Alaska. Your main cruise lines in Alaska are Princess and Holland America; there is a healthy competition for the Alaska cruise passenger between these two cruise lines, and they both have several ships plying the Inside Passage and Alaskan coast up to Whittier (or Seward). The other cruise lines may have one or two ships offering Alaska itineraries, but I try to stick to my preferred supplier up in Alaska, only because they have been doing it for so long, own many of the busses and tour companies that offer the shore excursions, and have the advantage of longevity up there.

I would call and order the major cruise lines, including Princess Cruises, Royal Caribbean, Holland America (if you have a lot of older passengers), Disney Cruise Lines (you will hopefully have people asking about Disney…pick up some resort brochures as well, just in case), Celebrity Cruise Lines, Norwegian Cruise Line and any of the Luxury cruise lines you think you may want to sell. I keep Oceania, Azamara, Viking and Crystal Cruises brochures in my files. You can also call Viking River Cruises and Avalon Cruises to have some river cruise catalogs on file. These are just suggestions; please do some research and see if there are any other cruise lines you may want to sell.

So, now that you've ordered your brochures and started on your deck plan binder, how do you read these deck plans?

READING A DECK PLAN

Let's start with a very simple deck plan, just to get your feet wet. You can find a full-color deck plan of the *Pacific Princess* on my website at www.howtosellcruises.com. (Due to publishing restrictions, we are unable to print the color deck plan in the book.)

This is one of Princess Cruises "small ships," which they acquired from the now-defunct Renaissance Cruises. The room categories have been changed as of May 2013, but I want to start with the older category delineations, just to get you used to the typical configuration of a ship. (Please see Princess Cruises' course in POLAR online that talks about the new re-grading of the ship to understand their new category changes. It is quite extensive, so it's best that you learn about it through Princess' own teaching portal.)

The decks go from lowest to highest. The lower the number of the deck, the lower it is on the ship. Typically the cruise line will start with the lowest passenger deck as deck 1, 2, or 3. There may be three or four more decks below that, but they are crew quarters and passengers are not allowed in these areas. Every cruise line displays their decks differently; some start with their lowest deck on the far left, some have it on the far right. Princess has Deck 3 on the far right of the second page, and this is the lowest passenger deck, with a few ocean-view staterooms. There may even be crew staterooms down on these lower decks; every ship is different.

You can see that there are several colors on the deck plan. Each color represents a different category. The first category and color I would like to look at is the magenta staterooms found on Deck 8, along the inside corridor of the ship. These are category II (double I), and are considered interior staterooms. As explained above, they have no windows or portholes, and are the least expensive staterooms on the ship. Category II are the most expensive of the interior staterooms, only because they are up on the highest passenger deck.

There is a perceived notion that the higher up the staterooms are, the better they are. This stems from the very early days of cruising (1800s and early 1900s) when the seas were smelly and there was no air conditioning. You wanted to be higher up so you could take advantage of the cool ocean breezes through open windows, but be located up away from the smells of the sea. The perception stuck, so now you will usually find the more expensive staterooms on the higher decks. In the beginning days of Mass Market cruising (1970s and early 1980s), you either had an interior stateroom, ocean-view stateroom, or deluxe stateroom. In the latter part of the 20th century, the marketing departments of cruise lines realized that they could make more money by pricing the higher level staterooms more expensively than the lower level staterooms, even though the experience, amenities, and room size were exactly the same. Thus the myriad of categories were born!

The *Oasis* class ships hold the record with forty-four different categories! Some category assignments make no sense on these ships; for example, a balcony room on one deck is exactly the same in size, layout, and amenities as the room next door, and yet it is considered a different and more expensive category. The only thing I can see is that the more expensive cabin of the two is a three- or four-berthed stateroom, so the first and second passengers pay significantly more than their neighbors for the privilege of being able to accommodate their family in the same room. Very smart, Royal Caribbean! (But, sad for families with small children who have to pay more.)

Back to the *Pacific Princess*... Deck 7 has light blue and yellow interior staterooms, and these are less expensive than those up on Deck 8. They may be exactly the same in size, amenities, and cruising experience, but it is a "perceived" benefit to be up on Deck 8. Some people think there is less movement the higher up you are. Actually, the least amount of movement can be found right in the middle of the ship, so on this vessel, the least amount of movement would be found amidships on decks 5 or 6. Unfortunately, these decks do not have inside staterooms, so Deck 7 would probably have less movement than Deck 8, and yet the perception is Deck 8 is more desirable. See how the marketing department increases profits just by pricing? Brilliant! Personally, I feel very claustrophobic in interior staterooms, so I would book one of the obstructed ocean view staterooms on Deck 6 before I would book an interior stateroom. Quite often, the lowest priced obstructed ocean-view stateroom will be priced the same, or sometimes even less than, the highest priced interior room! Go figure.

Speaking of obstructed view, the *Pacific Princess* does have two categories of obstructed ocean-view staterooms, categories GG and G. These are found on Deck 6, and are goldenrod and light blue in color. As you can see, there are lifeboats in front of these staterooms. In most cases, the obstruction is close to 100%, but there is some natural light that comes through the windows, so these staterooms are less claustrophobic than the interior staterooms. These rooms can often be a good deal price-wise for the budget-minded traveler. I know of a couple that takes the world cruise every year in one of these staterooms. They could not manage sailing in an interior room for 112 days, but the obstructed view room suits them just fine, and is less expensive than the traditional ocean-view staterooms.

The ocean-view staterooms are found down on decks 3 and 4, and are purple, lavender, and marine blue, respectively. (There are two other ocean-view categories called "Deluxe Ocean View", which basically means these staterooms are larger, but there are only two of each category up on decks 6 and 7; category CC and C.) It seems that on the newer ships, most of the ocean-view staterooms are located on the lower passenger decks. There is such a demand for balcony staterooms that it appears the ocean-view rooms have become almost obsolete and are relegated to the lower decks. Remember that it is a marketing ploy to make the staterooms on the higher decks more expensive, and thus more desirable. The only downside to being this close to the waterline is possibly hearing the anchor as it rises and falls from the ship, and also hearing the sound of the waves as the ship sails. One other possibility is hearing the bow thrusters when the ship is pulling into port; these thrusters help the Captain "park" the ship at the pier, kind of like parallel parking. Noise can be a problem in any part of the ship, so it is really hard to know without having sailed in one of these staterooms. If these particular noises exist, they are only a problem for a very brief time; i.e., when pulling into port or leaving port. The sound of the waves can actually be very relaxing, so hopefully if the stateroom is down on the lowest deck, the passengers would actually think this a benefit to their location.

Going back to the deck plan, the next category we will look at is the balcony stateroom. Let's look at category BF on decks 6 and 7. The deck plan key states that these are partially obstructed-view balcony staterooms. Looking at the location, these staterooms are very far forward or aft. When staterooms are in this location and are obstructed, it usually means from part of the architecture of the ship. Looking at a photo of the outside of the ship, the aft balconies have the ship's infrastructure blocking half of the view, and the forward balconies on Deck 7 seem to have obstruction from the bridge wing. I would not be surprised if these six category BF staterooms are actually mostly used as upgrades from ocean-view staterooms. Let us look at how upgrading works:

UPGRADING, "GUARANTEES," AND OVERSELLING

Cruise lines oversell ships all the time. They will oversell the lead-in price for each category type, then upgrade out of this lead-in category based on a number of things: past-passenger status (the more days sailed, the more chance of being upgraded), earliest bookings (the earlier your passenger books, the more likely an upgrade), if they are part of a group (if the cruise line needs twelve staterooms in category BF upgraded, and you have twelve staterooms booked and under final payment in that category on a guarantee basis, the coordinator of the ship may upgrade the entire group, thus solving their problem in one fell swoop, providing you did not check the box in their booking saying not to upgrade them), or any number of other factors. Thus, you may see ten beds available in category K, ten in category G and ten in category BF, even though the ship is almost sold out. The cruise line will then show that there are no available stateroom numbers to assign when booking in those categories, only guarantees. This enables the cruise line to sell a category type, and then berth everyone at a later date by upgrading them.

What is a guarantee? A guarantee means that your client is "guaranteed" a stateroom in the category they have booked, or a higher category and/or stateroom type. The downside is that you are unable to determine whether or not they are forward, aft, or midship at the time of booking. The upside is that more often than not, they will be upgraded to a higher category, making you look like a star to your clients! (Princess Cruises has streamlined the upgrade process in their new grading system of their ships – please take their class on POLAR online to see how they have done so.)

My point is that even though there are only six staterooms (or twelve berths) in category BF on this ship, very often Princess will sell something like thirty berths in that category. This allows passengers to book balconies at the lowest lead-in price, then upgrade them out of that category to a higher one. Because these have obstructed views, Princess might berth these upgrades in staterooms that might not be as in-demand, such as category BE, which are aft on Deck 6, or BD in forward or aft staterooms. As you can imagine, the midship staterooms are usually the first to be booked on a ship, so the forward and aft staterooms are the ones that are left to be upgraded into. (This actually used to be my job at Princess Cruises; berthing the ship and upgrading passengers based on the above criteria.) Each sailing is like a big puzzle, fitting passengers into the category type they have booked, or better; and overselling the lowest-priced of each category type (inside, ocean view, balcony) and then finding where to put them all. Cruise lines have made sophisticated computer programs to handle initial upgrading, but when it comes time to finalize a sailing, it is often up to a human coordinator to ensure everyone is taken care of and there are enough berths to go around.

Don't be surprised if one day you get a call from one of these coordinators a week prior to sailing, offering your clients a huge incentive to move over to another similar or better sailing because the ship is oversold and they did not get enough cancellations. The typical statistic is that a cabin is sold 2 to 3 times during the "life" of a sailing, what with cancellations up until the final payment. As mentioned before, cancellation penalties start accruing at final payment, so passengers can cancel for any reason up until this date. Now, some of the cruise lines are selling insurance policies that allow passengers to cancel *for any reason* up until sailing if they take the cruise line's insurance. This gives the passenger even more chance to capriciously cancel their cruise. Thus, the overselling policy of the cruise lines, which can be very frustrating to the ship's coordinator and to a passenger who is on a guarantee basis and is awaiting their stateroom assignment.

Assigned staterooms are when you book your client in a particular category and choose a stateroom from that category. There are several reasons you might want to choose a stateroom at the time of booking: desire to be in a specific location (midship is usually considered to be the best), family members booking two or more staterooms wanting to be next to each other, adjoining staterooms (a door between the two staterooms found within the cabin), necessity of three or four (or in the case of Disney, five) berths to accommodate a larger family, the list goes on. If you are booking a triple or quad, typically the cruise line will not allow you to book a guarantee. They will require you to actually choose a stateroom to ensure you have the proper amount of beds needed for your party. If there are no triple or quad staterooms available to book into, then that category will usually show sold out, even though there are stateroom numbers available in that same category that can accommodate two passengers. It is rare that you are able to hold a triple or quad without a specific stateroom number; the only time I've seen this happen is when every stateroom in that category holds triples and/or quads and they are counting on upgrading others out of that category in order to make room for your passengers. It is important to book as early as possible if your clients will need triples or quads, as they are usually the first to sell out.

I have also seen situations where there are triples and quads available to sell into, but the ship is closed to any additional triples and quads being sold. We usually find this situation around the holidays when lots of families are traveling. This is because the ship has met its lifeboat capacity for third and fourth berths and cannot safely accept any more due to regulations. So, the ship may have a lifeboat capacity for 1,500 first and second passengers, and 500 third and fourth passengers, but actually have 600 third and fourth berths in the stateroom configurations in order to give maximum flexibility when it comes to berthing families. The cruise line just has to keep a close watch on the numbers, and closes off the sailing to third and fourth berths once they reach the capacity for lifeboats. Better safe than sorry!

Should you leave a booking on a guarantee if there are actual stateroom numbers available? That is up to you. If it is a category that only has a few actual staterooms, but is a lead-in category (see above), and the actual rooms are not in the best location, or perhaps have an obstruction, then yes, I would leave it as a guarantee. The worst scenario is that they actually berth your clients in the category they booked; but it is likely that they will be upgraded to another category and receive a room in a better location.

It is important to advise your client that they could be berthed in that category, and tell them the location may not be ideal; if they want to ensure they get a better located stateroom, they should book and pay for the lowest category they are willing to actually sail in. You don't want to ever promise upgrades, even if they are on a guarantee basis with no stateroom numbers available. You never know when the ship's coordinator may upgrade someone who is already booked in a stateroom and slide your passenger into that room. Honesty is the best policy, and your mantra *has* to be "no surprises at embarkation"!

LOCATION, LOCATION, LOCATION

We have talked about midship being the best location on the ship as far as the least amount of movement, but what about other considerations?

Here are just a few hints that I have accumulated over the years.

I usually try to not book the very top passenger deck if the staterooms are right below the pool deck. The scraping of deck chairs being dragged about the deck can sometimes be heard in the cabins below. Also, if the staterooms are immediately under the buffet, there is a lot of chair scraping and heavy footfall by crew members preparing all of the meals and setting tables. Sometimes this is the only deck the suites are located on, so you might not have a choice, but if I can help it, I will always try for decks that have other passenger staterooms above them rather than public areas. The same goes for staterooms that are located immediately underneath entertainment venues. Often the music goes into the wee hours of the morning, and if I have light sleepers, the cabins immediately underneath these show lounges can be affected. You are usually safe if the venue is the grand theatre where the Broadway-style revue shows are produced, as they are finished by 10:30 p.m. It's the lounges where the bands play that can be tricky, usually found in the aft end of the ship. (Again, check the deck plans as each ship is different.) On the *Pacific Princess*, all of the mini-suites are up on Deck 8, so you have no choice but to book them underneath the pool deck, but I would try for rooms under the Internet Café or Card Room, not the fitness center, if I had a choice of staterooms.

We briefly spoke of staterooms near the water line; check with your clients to see if the noise of the sea would keep them awake or not. The staterooms down on Deck 3 will definitely hear the water. For some people, this is very relaxing, but for others, it might keep them up at night. The lower staterooms will also hear the bow thrusters when pulling into and out of ports. If you clients like to sleep in, this might be a problem. The hope is that they are up and ready to go ashore, so this point would hopefully be moot. But if they tell you they are not going ashore and like to sleep in, they might need to think of booking balcony staterooms on the upper decks, or staterooms on Deck 4 rather than Deck 3. Bow thrusters are found far forward and far aft. They help the ship to push in and out of port by water displacement, and can tend to make the ship shake a bit. The smaller the ship, the more these lower staterooms will feel them. The anchor can also be heard on the lower decks; some ships have them forward, some aft, so it depends on the ship. I've only ever had a problem once, and that was when I was all the way aft on the very lowest passenger deck, but I learned to look forward to hearing the chain lower and raise; it reminded me that I was on a ship, and made me feel secure in our position.

If I had to choose forward or aft, I usually prefer all the way aft looking over the back end of the ship. I love watching the wake of the ship as we make our way through the ocean or sea. If your passenger has a balcony, they will love it even more. I have a couple who will only book the very farthest aft staterooms because now they sit on their balcony, cocktails in hand, and just relax watching the sea as it spreads out behind them. Lovely!

Always try to sell a balcony room. The enjoyment your passengers will receive is worth the extra $100 or $200 it may cost them. But, if it's the difference (inside or outside vs. balcony) between going or not going, then make them feel confident in their decision to go, no matter what the stateroom type.

WHEELCHAIR-ACCESSIBLE STATEROOMS AND THE DISABLED PASSENGER

About a quarter of my clients are in a wheelchair, so I have become quite adept in booking cruises for passengers who need accessible staterooms. Fortunately for my clients, the cruise lines have worked very hard at making cruising available to people with disabilities, even going so far as to creating departments whose sole responsibility is to take care of those who need special care while onboard the ship.

We can thank Jan Tuck at Princess Cruises for spearheading this movement. She is so respected in the cruising industry that she was appointed by President George W. Bush as head of the U.S. Access Board. While she was in office, the Access Board drew up guidelines that the cruise lines have to implement to help those who need a little extra help. This includes not only access for people in wheelchairs, but also the blind, hard of hearing, and those with other disabilities. She once shared with me about a cruise that had more than twenty-five guide dogs accompanying their sight-impaired masters; her department had prepared specially made dog biscuits to be put on each doggie bed every night, similar to their owner's pillow chocolates! She also made sure there was sufficient plots of grass for the dogs to "do their business," as well as a myriad of other details that ensured the cruise went smoothly for their owners. They all had a marvelous time!

The most important element in all of this is that there are now staterooms that can safely and comfortably accommodate wheelchairs and motorized scooters. Every detail, from the widths of the doors to wheel-in showers, grab bars in the bathrooms, and dressers and closets that are within reach of a person in a chair has been thought of. But this is an emerging area in cruising, so there is still a lot to be done. Jan and I do ship inspections all the time and find lots of areas that still need improvement, but the cruise industry is at least moving forward in this area.

The reason I spend so much time talking about this is because I want you to be aware of the importance of leaving these staterooms for those who truly need them. I've seen many passengers who have reserved these staterooms just because they are larger in size, but they don't really need the amenities these staterooms provide. I've also tried to book clients on voyages where every single wheelchair stateroom had been reserved over a year and a half in advance, but we were not sure if those that were booked were actually confined to wheelchairs. Please be courteous and only book these rooms if your client is in a wheelchair or scooter. If your client can actually walk, but uses a scooter to get around just because they don't feel like exerting the energy to walk, call the cruise line. They can advise you if there are other rooms available that will allow your passengers to park their scooter out of the way to charge the battery, but not necessarily take an accessible stateroom just because it's larger. If we all follow the guidelines, then those rooms will be available to those who truly need them. Thank you!

If you have a passenger who is disabled, it is vital that you let the cruise line know as much as possible prior to embarkation so they can be prepared. Most of the cruise lines now have a questionnaire to be filled out prior to sailing that details the passenger's needs and restrictions. Cruise lines can now handle dietary restrictions (including gluten free, dairy-free, etc.), oxygen, and of course, all ships have a fully equipped medical center should any medical attention be needed. (However, if they need oxygen, they will need to arrange to have it delivered to the ship using an approved vendor that the cruise line has approved.) Whenever I have needed to arrange a scooter, wheelchair, or oxygen for my passenger, I have used Special Needs at Sea. They deliver to most U.S. ports. Again, please check with the cruise line to see who they recommend.

The one thing they cannot handle onboard is dialysis. Contact the cruise lines if this is an issue, because in the past there have been cruises for dialysis patients where they bring the equipment onboard. The cruise line might know of who to contact for this unusual situation; I have not seen a dialysis cruise for many years, but that does not mean they still do not take place.

If your passenger is sight-impaired, they will need to bring their own caregiver. (They will need to pay for his/her accommodation.) If they have a guide dog, special arrangements will need to be made through the cruise line.

In the past, some of the cruise lines have provided interpreters for deaf passengers, but this is something you would need to call the cruise line to find out. I've seen two different scenarios: In the first, the interpreters were provided by the cruise line; in the second, the guest had to bring her own, but the cruise line helped with the accommodation.

If your passenger needs a caregiver, it is their responsibility to bring their own, and pay for accommodation for them. I've always just booked an inside stateroom across the hall (or as close as possible) if they are not sharing the same cabin.

One of the most important things to advise your clients in scooters and wheelchairs is that it is very likely they will be unable to disembark in "tender" ports. A *tender* is a small boat that is used to take passengers from the ship to the shore when the ship is too large to pull into a dock. In these cases, the ship sits out in the harbor and the tender boats go back and forth, shuttling passengers to shore side. If your client is in a scooter, these scooters are extremely heavy, and it's impossible to take them off the ship when there is a small gangway that leads to a boat. Often, the water is quite rough, and it is very dangerous to try and carry someone in a chair down the gangway that is likely casting about with the waves. I know this can be quite upsetting to someone confined to a chair, but ultimately it is their safety that the cruise line is concerned about. It is always up to the Captain of the ship whether he will allow his crew members to carry someone in their wheelchair down the tender gangway and onto the boat. He (or she...Royal Caribbean has a female Captain!) will weigh all the different factors, including how rough the water is, how steep the gangway is, how much the person and their equipment weighs, how difficult will it be shore side, and the likelihood of getting them back to the ship. I make it very clear in their invoice that wheelchairs are not allowed ashore in tender ports; then, if the cruise line is able to do so, it's icing on the cake for them.

Cruise lines also now have wheelchair-accessible shore excursions (in non-tendered ports), so be sure to check those out with your client prior to the cruise to see what is offered. Sometimes there are wheelchair-accessible vans that are available for private tours, so that might be their best option.

If your client is taking the cruise line's transfers to and from the ship, it is your responsibility to make sure the cruise line is aware of their disability and whether they need a wheelchair-accessible vehicle for the transfer. One would hope the cruise line would read the notes on the booking, but this is not always the case. When I first started booking passengers and POLAR had just been introduced, I had a client who needed wheelchair-accessible transportation. I had not called Princess to tell them he was in a chair, so the code delineating that he was in a chair was never put on the file, since there is no way to do so in POLAR. (To this day you still need to call Princess, Holland America, and Cunard to tell them to put the code on the file showing that a client uses chair full time; it is not automatically done when you reserve an accessible stateroom.) They almost didn't make it to the ship because there was no way to get them into the steep van they were using for transfers. Eventually they had three guys carry him onto the van, and drove his motorized chair in a separate vehicle, but it was touch and go for an hour, and he was deeply upset by it.

DECK PLANS OF OTHER CRUISE LINES

We have used Princess Cruises' *Pacific Princess* to discuss how to read a deck plan. Other cruise lines are very similar. I suggest investing in a magnifying glass and keeping it next to your work area; some of the deck plans are almost illegible because their stateroom numbers are so small! As mentioned before, some of the cruise lines are no longer printing brochures, so you will need to print their deck plans. What is nice about online deck plans is they can sometimes be interactive; when you or your client clicks on their stateroom, it may pull up a photo of the room, the location in relation to elevators, etc., and the view from the window. Deck plans will occasionally change (Princess Cruises re-graded all of their ships), so please make sure you are looking at the most recent version. I recall a few years ago when the Solstice Class ships came out from Celebrity Cruises; their original deck plans of the Celebrity Solstice showed an entire deck of regular balcony staterooms. Once they took delivery of the ship, they noticed that all the staterooms on this particular deck had obstructions on the bottom half of every balcony! They had to re-grade these staterooms to show the obstruction. Had I not looked online at their deck plan, I would have sold these staterooms as regular balcony rooms. Needless to say, I would have had very unhappy clients once they embarked the ship! (It was a group of eight staterooms, all booking balconies in a row…that would have been a lot of unhappy people!) Sometimes in the early days of your cruise-selling career, it helps to talk over stateroom selection with a reservation agent at the cruise line. They very often have insight that you might not have, just because they work with these ships on a daily basis. Don't be afraid to ask questions – there are no stupid questions! – only disappointed passengers if you don't do your due diligence!

Organizing Your Office

WHETHER YOU ARE A brand new travel agent or a seasoned one, organizing your paperwork can be one of the single most daunting tasks in your business. Believe me, I know! I've been doing this for more than thirty-five years and it still thwarts me. The thing I've found to be most effective is having a system in place so that you always know where to look each day as you begin your work, and a checks-and-balances system that reminds you of each task needed for each booking. This chapter will hopefully help you create a system that works for you, and give you the tools necessary so you won't have to reinvent the wheel.

WHAT YOU WILL NEED

I find the easiest way to organize my booking sheets is in a binder. When I first started, a 1" three-ring binder was adequate for the number of booking sheets I had; as my business grew, I found I needed to expand that to 1½" and now a 2", but in the beginning, a 1" should suffice and won't be too cumbersome for you.

Other items you will need:

- Monthly tabs – for your binder – so you can separate booking sheets by month.
- Three-hole punch.

- Colored file folders – I prefer the multicolored pack that includes blue, red, orange, green, and yellow.
- File folder labels.
- Calendar for writing final payments and other deadlines (computer is fine).
- Cruise Reservation Form (sample on page 148) copied on colored paper
- Avery Big Tab Insertable Plastic Single Pocket Dividers.
- Oxford Twin pocket folders for your deposit packets.

You can find master copies of all these forms at www.howtosellcruises.com/forms.html. (It's important to include html at the end of the URL, otherwise you won't be able to pull up the forms.) Depending on how busy your business is, you will want to make enough to last you for several months. I currently have my cruise forms on lavender and group forms on blue. This helps me differentiate which type of booking when the forms are in the binder. Hole punch these before you store them so you don't have to worry about doing so with each booking.

Insert the monthly tabs in your binder. I also use the Avery Plastic Single Pocket Tab Dividers to hold miscellaneous papers, including your commission forms, so you can insert those at the front of the binder as well.

Make three copies of the commission report (page 147) and mark one for this year and one for next year. The third should be marked Other, and will be used for any other commissionable travel you book, including hotels, car rentals etc. These can be on white paper. Slide those in the first pocket so they are right in front. I use these to not only track my commissions, but also if I need to find a particular booking – it gives me a quick view of what month to look in.

You can start by taking each existing booking you already have and transfering the information to a new booking sheet. This will give you a uniform way of keeping track of all of your bookings.

BOOKING SHEETS

Let's take a look at these in detail. Most of the fields are self-explanatory, but some areas may need clarification.

CRUISE RESERVATION FORM

Names____________________DOB________
_________________________DOB________
_________________________DOB________
_________________________DOB________
Address______________________________
City________________St______ZIP______
Ph(h)______________Cel_______________
Air City____________C/O Y or N
Source of booking_______________________
Email ______________________________

"Names" should be their *full* names as they appear on the clients' passports. "DOB" is date of birth. *Always* ask the DOB when you are booking. Almost all companies, whether airline, tour, or cruise company will require this. "Air City" is followed by "C/O," which means Cruise Only. Many of my clients are doing their own air, so I just circle Y if the cruise line is *not* doing their air, or N if we are using the cruise line's air. (I know, this seems backwards. If it is too confusing, you can change to the other way for your own use!) "Source of Booking" is very important...this is who you need to thank for this referral, or to note if they found you online, etc. Finally, "E-mail Address" for me is imperative. A good 98% of my business is done via e-mail, so if they do not have an e-mail address, I note this here.

Sailing Date________Res#___________
Res Agent_________Voy/Grp#_________
Date Booked____________________

This box, found in the upper righthand corner, is the main information of the booking. If I made the reservation on POLAR or Cruising Power, etc., I mark that under "Res Agent."

"Voy/Grp#" refers to the Voyage number given by Princess, HAL, and Cunard. The group number is important to note if your booking falls into a group, even if you personally haven't booked that group. Often, your host agency will have a group on that sailing, and your booking will automatically be a part of it (particularly on Princess, HAL, and Cunard). The "Date Booked" is also important, as insurance companies ask for this whenever you make a claim. It also can affect fees that are charged to the client; if they book prior to the addition of a particular fee, *sometimes* knowing the date booked can be advantageous to your client not having to pay that fee.

Dining: Early	Late	PC	Confirmed	W/L
Table Size 2 4 6 8				
Seating with________				
Special Diet________				
Special Occasion________				

"Dining" refers to early seating, late seating, or PC (which is Personal Choice, As You Wish, Freestyle, or whatever the cruise line calls it). I also circle whether it is confirmed or waitlisted, so I can follow up if they are waitlisted. In the "Seating With" section, you should not only put the names of the others they are traveling with, but if they are with Princess, Cunard, or HAL, you can obtain a Traveling With ID (TWID) code. This is a three-number/letter code that alerts the cruise line to those who are traveling together. You can actually request this when you are making your bookings online, on the last page. The TWID code is then found under Important Notes on the booking summary. If there is a special diet or occasion, I will not only mark it here, but also put the date and how I alerted the cruise line; i.e., POLAR 11/1/10 or Kathy 11/1/10. If it doesn't have a name and date, then I know I did not tell the cruise line.

Cruise Line________		Ship________	
Destination________		#Nts________	
Cat________	Gtee________	Cbn#________	
Inside	Outside	Balc	Suite
________			
Air Dept Date________		Rtn________	
Ports from/to________			

This is fairly self-explanatory. If they book a guaranteed stateroom, I put a check here, and then when the cabin is assigned, I will write it in. I circle the type of stateroom, and there is also space to write any other information you might need.

The "Air Departure Date" is important because if the cruise starts in Europe, Asia, Australia, etc., your air departure date is completely different than the cruise departure date.

"Return" is also important if they've added on a post-cruise hotel package or they have decided to stay on themselves. If they add a pre- or post-hotel package, I will use the back of the booking sheet to write the information; i.e., name of the hotel, number of nights, etc. I will know there is a hotel package through the cruise line because there will be a fare entered in the fare column under Land. I will also write out passenger's air schedules on the back.

FARE			TOTALS	C/L GROSS
Fare	______	x___	=______	______
Disc	______	x___	=______	______
Sell	______	x___	=______	______
3/4	______	x___	=______	______
Air	______	x___	=______	______
Land	______	x___	=______	______
Insur	______	x___	=______	______
AL HT	______	x___	=______	______
Fuel	______	x___	=______	______
Port	______	x___	=______	______
Govt	______	x___	=______	______
Trf	______	x___	=______	______
Other	______	x___	=______	______
TOT	______	X___	=______	______
COM				______

Here is where the money information goes. Column 1 is the per-person rate.

Column 2 is how many to multiply the amount in Column 1 (i.e., x2 for the first two passengers in the stateroom). Column 3 is the total after multiplying. Column 4 is left empty until the very final payment. This is where I put what the cruise line is showing in the computer. I pride myself in going the extra mile for my clients, so I am constantly price checking online for them. For more than 70% of my clients, I can usually bring their cruise fares down from the time they book to the time they cruise. All these price changes can make for a messy booking form sometimes! This last column is where the *final* figures go, so I have an accurate amount for my clients.

Often I like to show my clients if there is a discount that I can offer them, so the first "Fare" field is the brochure fare or pre-discounted fare. "Disc" is the discount we can offer them and "Sell" is what they are paying after the discount. I personally quote the cruise fare less the port tax, or non commissionable fare (NCF). Some cruise lines include NCF's in their cruise fare. I always subtract it out as I like to show them the true cruise fare before the Non-Commissionable Fare. I then put the port taxes below in "Port."

"3/4" refers to passenger 3 or 4, and what their cruise fare is prior to port taxes.

"Air" is where you would put their airfare if they choose to take air from the cruise line. If there are separate air taxes, I put down in the row designated "Other."

"Land" is for any land packages (e.g., hotels, pre-cruise tours, etc.) that are taken from the cruise line. If they book through another tour company for pre- or post-cruise arrangements, *I fill out a separate tour form, as the commission is coming from another source and not the cruise line.*

"Insur" is for insurance purchased *through the cruise line.* I will always price out the cruise line insurance and my alternative travel company (e.g. Travel Guard or Travelex) and offer both. At the bottom of the "Fare" ladder is where you put the alternative insurance information.

Travel Ins. ____________________	Coverage pp____________
Purchased:______________________________	Y or N

"Travel Ins." is the name of the policy quoted (e.g., Basic, Select), and coverage per person at which you priced it. If they decide to purchase this alternative insurance, then put the date you processed the policy. *Only* put a date here if you have a confirmed policy from the insurance company. If they give you a definitive *no*, then circle N. Hopefully, if there is an N here, there is an amount up above in the "Insur" field! Try to *never* have a client not be insured. I have too many horror stories to share, and they're always about those clients who have categorically refused coverage! I also have stories where there was no way the clients could have afforded the benefits they received had they not taken the insurance.

"AL HT" is a totally optional field for the Alaska Head Tax. This may be confusing for those who are new in the business. Several years ago, Alaska initiated a tax of $50 per person. In the early days of the head tax, we had to add it on to their cruise price. This field is now obsolete, but I keep it in case they decide to add it back in again.

"Fuel" is a field we hopefully never have to use again. Years ago, the cruise lines charged $9 to $11 per day for a fuel supplement. Their thought was that rather than raising the cruise fares to cover the fuel, it would be a better marketing strategy to keep the cruise fares low and add on a fuel supplement. It was a disaster, prompting many lawsuits and unhappy passengers. They are warning us that we have to advise our clients that these fuel supplements could be reinstated at any time; thus we have this field.

"Port" is the aforementioned Port Tax, which I always subtract out and add in here.

"Govt" is Government Fees, also known as Taxes and Fees on the cruise confirmations. "Trf" is for transfers taken from the cruise line. These are sometimes called Packages or Mods on the cruise line's confirmations, but always refer to transfers to and from the ship that the passenger has to pay extra for.

"Other" is a field for any other charges you may need to add on. "Total" is the total of each column.

"Comm" is for commission; I put the amount that is paid to me from the cruise line here. Once I get paid from my host agency, Montrose Travel (MT), I circle it on this form showing I received it, and write in the actual amount MT sent me underneath.

PAYMENT INFORMATION
Deposit pp__________x_____=_________
Option date______________extend________
Balance due $__________________________
Final Pymt date KC_________C/L_________
Dep
CC#____________________**Exp**______
Name____________________**code**______
FP____________________Exp______
Name____________________code______
AMX Platinum tracking:______________to:

Finally we come to the payment information. You have the deposit per person, the option date that the deposit is due, and if you need to extend it, put the new date here. The "Final Payment" field shows when I need it in my office ("KC") and when it is due to the cruise line ("C/L"). I will usually put 5 days prior to the due date to the cruise line. Now that the cruise lines are getting so strict with the final payment due dates, make sure to give yourself enough time, and let your passengers know you will charge their final payment at the time you have put payment due to KC. (KC stands for Kensington Cruises, in case you were wondering!)

"Dep" stands for Deposit; often clients will use different credit cards for the deposit and for final payment, so I put two fields here. There is room for the credit card number, the expiration date, the full name on the card, and the three- or four-digit code found on the back (front for American Express). Then, the "FP" is if there is a different card for the final payment. If the client okays the deposit card for the final payment, I will write in the FP field, "okay to use above card."

Many cruise lines have a special amenity program with American Express if the client pays *all* payments with a *platinum* American Express Card. If a client gives me an American Express card, I always ask what type of card it is: blue, gold, or platinum. It needs to be a true platinum card, and not through Costco or any other consortium. You will need to log on to the AMX travel agent website at www.americanexpress.com/asdonline where you can get a tracking number. If you are part of a host agency, they will have to give you their code. Once you are logged in, you will click on the tab on the lefthand side, "Add new booking," and follow the instructions. If the card is eligible for a tracking number, it will pull up a screen to input all the information about the cruise. (You will need to click on "cruise" on the top righthand side of the screen to access the cruise input screen.) You may enter up to two separate booking numbers for each American Express platinum card. You will receive a six-digit tracking number preceded by two letters (designating the cruise line). I write that tracking number in this last field. Unfortunately, you are not done yet; you need to call the cruise line's reservations department and give this tracking number to a reservation agent. Some cruise lines always accept the tracking number and offer the amenities, and some offer it only with specific fares. Regent, HAL, and Crystal Cruises usually offers them with all fares, but unfortunately Princess does not, so I do not let my clients know if they are even eligible for them until I have verbal confirmation from Princess. The list of cruise lines that offers American Express amenities are as follows:

Supplier Name
Holland America Line
Princess Cruises
Windstar Cruises
Regent Seven Seas Cruises
Cunard Line
Crystal Cruises
Silversea Cruises
Seabourn
Royal Caribbean International
Celebrity Cruises
Uniworld
Oceania Cruises
Azamara Cruises

Some amenities might be a $300 to $500 onboard credit per stateroom or a combination of offerings. For example, Princess currently offers a $300-per-stateroom shipboard credit for suites or two-category upgrade within stateroom type for inside, outside, balcony, and mini-suite staterooms; *plus* dinner in one of the specialty dining venues for the first night of cruise; *plus* a bottle of champagne.

I will write the name of the reservation agent and the date I gave them the tracking number in this very bottom corner.

The most important part of this booking sheet is *this box*.

Dep In House	________	$________
Dep remitted	________	To________
Mtravel comp	________	
Dep pkt sent	________	
Adv returned	________	
F/P reminder	________	
FP remitted	________	To________
Mtravel comp	________	
Docs in	________	
Docs checked	________	
Bon Voy gift	________	To________
Gift________	________	$________
Docs sent	________	
Welcome home	________	
Res cxld	________	To________

This is where I keep on top of my bookings, and is an invaluable tool on staying organized. It's fairly self-explanatory, but here is how I use it.

The first column is for dates.

"Dep In House" is the date the deposit is in house and the amount of deposit.

"Dep remitted" is the date I remitted it to the cruise line and the name of the agent, or POLAR, or "CP" for Cruising Power, etc.

The next field, "Mtravel comp," is important if you are a member of a host agency. This is the date I let my host agency know about my booking by filling out a booking form on their website. Your host agency will probably have their own method of advising them of your booking. If you are not a member of a host agency, you can ignore this field.

If this field is not filled out, I know I goofed and won't get paid!

"Dep pkt sent": I personally send out a deposit packet whenever a client books a cruise with me. You should be sending one out as well – if not an actual packet, then have your invoices and Reservation Authorizations sent to them via e-mail. We discussed these on page 81. This is the date I sent the deposit packet.

"Adv rtnd" is for the date the clients returned their Reservation Authorization form back to me. *It is vitally important that I receive this back in the office.*

It is confirmation that they read my enclosed terms and conditions, and that all spellings are correct on their documents. Heaven forbid you are sued and don't have anything in writing from your clients showing that you did advise them of everything they needed to know. We will discuss voyage files later, but this is where I notate that I did receive it back and that it can be found in their voyage file.

- "F/P reminder" is the date I e-mailed them, or called them to remind that final payment is now due.
- "F/P remitted" is the date I remitted their final payment, and who I remitted it to. Again, if it is POLAR or CP, then I notate that as well.
- "Mtravel comp" is once again when I advise my host agency that final payment has been made.
- "Docs in" and "Docs checked" has become somewhat obsolete…now that everything is done as e-docs, the cruise lines don't send anything out anymore. I, however, go the extra mile, and will go online and make sure everything is

filled out, all the T's are crossed and I's are dotted, and print their boarding passes. I then package them up with some goodies and send them to my passenger. So this field is for me to designate the date I went online, printed their boarding passes, and checked to make sure all the immigration information is filled out.

- "Bon Voy gift" is for any Bon Voyage gifts I might send through the cruise line. I write the date I ordered them and the name of the agent I ordered them from (or POLAR or CP if done online). The next three lines are to say what exactly I did send and the dollar amount spent. Just a reminder: RCCL and Celebrity have discounted onboard gifts for travel agents to send to their clients, including wine and other goodies.
- The remaining fields are self explanatory. Hopefully you won't have to use the last one, but if you must cancel a reservation, make sure to note the date and the name of whom you cancelled with.

Once I've filled out the booking form, I need to remind myself on a daily basis about the "gotta do's" for that day. I personally keep a calendar right on top of my desk, and log in all final payment due dates, dates I should place gift orders, deposit dates, etc. I use it only for my cruise business, and I check it every day to see if there is anything I *have* to do today. This way I keep on top of my final payments and have it *right* in front of me! You can use your computer if you like, but I think it's important that it has an alarm to remind you to do things on a daily basis so you don't forget.

COMMISSIONS

So, now that you have your booking form all filled out, you can put it behind the appropriate month in your binder! Before you do, however, don't forget to log it on the commission report at the front.

This is fairly easy.... First, the "Cruise Line/Tour Co," then "Pax Name" (I write it out as last name, then first, to make it easier to find if I am looking for the passenger quickly.) For the "Sailing or departure Date," I usually write the sailing date even if they are leaving early for a pre-cruise package. The "Comm amount" is the commission amount *from the cruise line.* The amount I receive from my host agency is written under "Actual Amount" once I receive it. I also put a check mark under the "Rcvd" column once I receive it.

Now, here is how I use this report to make sure I receive my commissions and they are the correct amount. Once I've logged in my commissions from the cruise lines, checked off the ones I received, and written in the actual amount received, I go through my form and put a *circle* under "Rcvd" around the field of those commissions from that particular month that I have not received. For example, if I am double-checking the month of October, if there are any sailing dates from October that I did not have a check for, I put a circle in the Rcvd column. This alerts me to do some research on the status of that commission through the cruise line's website, or reservations. If the sailing is very late in the month, there is a good chance it just hasn't been sent to me. Usually I don't contact the cruise line until the next month that the commission goes unpaid, so I give them sixty days. If after sixty days there is no commission, then I contact accounting.

VOYAGE FILES

A voyage file (VF) is where you keep all of your paperwork and research for each client. I personally use a different color for each month:

- January - Blue
- February - Yellow
- March - Orange
- April - Green
- May - Red
- June - Blue

- July - Yellow
- August - Orange
- September - Green
- October - Blue
- November - Yellow
- December - Orange

Inside each file you should find:

- All correspondence sent to client, including copies of e-mails
- All research materials in conjunction with this booking
- Your completed Reservation Authorization
- Cruise line confirmations

You should keep these files for at least seven years. On the label I put the following:

- Top left: Passenger names, Last/First
- Top right: Sailing date
- Bottom left: Destination
- Bottom right: Ship and cruise line

These are filed *by date order* in my file drawer in my desk. I also have a filing cabinet in another part of my office – at the beginning of every month, I take all the VFs from two months ago and file them in a file drawer in the cabinet designated for this year. I have found that I usually need to refer to VFs up to two months after the sailing, but usually after that, it is okay to relegate it to the year drawer. I try to keep this year's and the previous year's VFs close at hand; at the end of the year, I will take all the VFs from two years ago and put them in a file box labeled with the year.

It is important to keep these in a safe place, as there is sensitive information inside, including credit card numbers, immigration information, and names with birth dates. Again, we need to keep our files for seven years for business purposes. I then professionally shred all documents once those seven years are up. (I have been known to dump all the contents into a big trash can to be shredded and reuse the colored folders, even though they are seven years old! Hey, nothing a file label can't take care of!) Once that drawer in my office is empty, it is ready for all the new files from the present year! This way, I always have an available drawer.

Checklist of a Cruise Booking

WE ARE NOW AT the end of the book. You've got your clients ready to cruise, now what do you do? Below is a checklist of steps for you to follow for each cruise booking. (Keep in mind this is *after* you have qualified them; i.e., determined which type of cruise line would be best for them, using the guidelines in CLIA's training course.)

- ❑ Determine destination
- ❑ Determine cruise line based on destination
    - Get price quotes for two or three different cruise lines and choose which one works for your client
- ❑ Determine stateroom type with your client: Suite, Mini Suite, Balcony, Ocean View, Interior?
- ❑ Questions to ask client:
    - The EXACT spelling of their names as they appear on their passports – no deviations!

      Note: If you are dealing with a honeymoon couple, the wife will use her maiden name that appears on her passport, as she won't have had time to get a new passport with her married name.

- Their birthdate?
- Dining choice? Early, Late, or Personal Choice/My Time Dining
- Cruise Line Insurance or Private Company Insurance. Always get the price from the cruise line in order to compare
- Do they want to book their air through the cruise line, or are they going to book their own?
- Do they want transfers from the cruise line? Pre, post, or both? (You can book transfers even if you do your own air. Just make sure they land within the time limits of when transfers take place).
- Do they want a hotel package through the cruise line? Pre, post, or both?
- Are they open to an upgrade from the cruise line? Or do they want the exact stateroom number you are reserving for them? On POLAR, there is a box to check if they do not want an upgrade, so it is important to let the cruise line know in advance.
- Are they traveling with anyone they know so you can cross-reference them for dining? If so, you will need to get the other booking numbers in order to advise the cruise line to cross-reference.
- *Always* ask if they can think of anyone else they know who might want to travel with them. I have gotten many new bookings this way!
- Are any of the passengers disabled in any way? Do they use a wheelchair or scooter to get around? Are they confined to the wheelchair or scooter, or can they walk and/

or ascend and descend stairs on their own? Are there any special dietary restrictions?

Now you are ready to either call the cruise line or sign onto the cruise line's reservation system to make the reservation.

Deposit: Always try to get the deposit on a credit card. As mentioned previously, it protects your client, and makes it easier for you to handle. If they insist on paying by cash or check, you will need to advise the cruise line, as it often takes more time to get your check to the cruise line than time you have with your option. You will have to send the check via overnight mail, so you may want to pass that expense on to your client. The cruise line will have you call in an agency check number in order to hold the booking. (If it is a Flash Fare, you will *have* to get a credit card for the deposit.) Most cruise lines will *not* allow you to use an agency credit card or your own personal credit card for payment, so bear that in mind. Deposits are due to the cruise line anywhere from the moment of booking to up to seven days from the time of booking.

As soon as the deposit is made, it is time to put together your deposit packet.

- ❑ Print down the "guest copy" of the invoice showing that the deposit has been made.
- ❑ Type up reservation authorization.
- ❑ Make sure to include Terms and Conditions.
- ❑ If a travel insurance company is being considered (other than the cruise line's policy) make sure to include a brochure from that company.
    - If client is using the cruise line's insurance policy, you may want to print the insurance brochure from the cruise line's website to include in the deposit packet. This is optional.

- ❑ Include a self-addressed-stamped-envelope for client to return the reservation authorization.
- ❑ Include a copy of the reservation authorization for the client to keep (in addition to the copy they are to send back).

FINAL PAYMENT

It is vitally important that you make your final payments on time, otherwise there is a good chance the cruise line will cancel your client's booking, even though there is money on the file! Put a note on your calendar for five to seven days prior to the due date to process that final payment. Again, try to encourage your client to pay with a credit card. If they insist on paying with cash or check, they must pay you at least two to three weeks prior to the due date, in order to give you time for their payment to clear your bank, and for you to get a check to the cruise line.

If they are taking the cruise line's insurance policy, you will pay for that with the final payment. If they do not take the cruise line's insurance policy, now is a good time to process the outside vendor's policy, because you are now entering into the cancellation penalty period with the cruise line. (That is, if they did not purchase the outside vendor's policy within twenty-one days of deposit. Some travel insurance companies will protect pre-existing conditions if a policy is purchased within 21 days of deposit. If they did not take advantage of this, then you need to process a policy at the same time as final payment so you are covered if something happens within the cancellation penalty period.)

I always make sure all the T's are crossed and I's are dotted when it comes to final payment time. Make sure you have addressed all items on the checklist *before* you get to the final payment date, just in case you need to make any changes. You *don't* want to be charged for changes that take place after the final payment date, especially for name spellings. If the client has a disability, make sure the cruise line has been advised of the nature of the disability. Some cruise lines have special forms to fill out; this is the time to ensure these forms have been done and sent back.

Final Payment Checklist

- ❑ Determine which insurance policy client has decided upon.
    - If the cruise line policy, pay for it with final payment
    - If alternative company, purchase soon after final payment has been made.
- ❑ Make sure cruise line is aware of any disabilities.
    - Ask cruise line if they have any specific forms to fill out, and complete them at this time.
- ❑ Make sure client has returned the reservation authorization no later than final payment time. If they have not, remind them you need it to complete their cruise booking. This protects you in the long run!
- ❑ Finalize any hotel bookings that may have been made separately.
- ❑ If you have helped client book air flights, finalize these, making sure you have seat assignments in accordance with their wishes.
    - Seat Guru.com is a great resource to determine which seats are best on every airplane and flight.

THREE WEEKS PRIOR TO SAILING

- ❑ Print boarding passes.
    - Client must have gone online prior to this to complete their immigration registration. If they have not completed this, you will need to call them to get the required information, such as passport number and emergency contact

information. At this point, you will need to fill out the online form, rather than waiting for them to complete it. Then, you will be able to print down the boarding passes.

- ❑ Mail boarding passes and baggage tags along with any other gifts (such as tote bags) that you wish to send.
- ❑ Process gift orders through the cruise line to be delivered onboard.

THE DAY BEFORE THEIR DEPARTURE

Call client to wish them BON VOYAGE! Remind them to bring their passports and cruise documentation! (Don't laugh…I forgot my passport on my last cruise!)

WHILE THEY ARE GONE

Send a note welcoming them back home. Remind them in the note that you are there for them when it comes time to book their next cruise.

Conclusion

So now you've got your system all set to keep on top of your bookings, payments, commissions, and even all that paperwork that goes with each booking. You know how to read a deck plan, and understand the different elements of a cruise booking as well as with some major differences in the cruise lines.

I hope this book has helped you start a system that will keep you on track, and that you will now be able to concentrate on building a successful travel business! You have all the tools and tricks of an experienced cruise-selling travel agent, so now it's up to you to start booking!

I wish you all the best in your venture and I'll see you on the high seas!

– Lori Berberian Pelentay

Appendix

DECK PLAN

Please go to www.howtosellcruises.com for a full color copy of the *Pacific Princess* deck plan.

FORMS

For full-sized copies of all the forms found in this Appendix, visit www.howtosellcruises.com/forms.html.

VENDORS

Baggage Tags

(plastic sleeves to fit printed bag tags)
Travelades
www.travelades.com
800-333-2774

Special Needs at Sea

(for wheelchair, scooter and oxygen rentals)
www.specialneedsatsea.com

BLOGS ABOUT CRUISING

(for more insights from Lori, check out her blogs)
Cruise With Lori
http://cruisewithlori.typepad.com/cruise_with_lori

Limiting Terms and Conditions

Kensington Cruises, hereinafter referred to as the Agency, issued this invoice in the sole capacity of agent for the owners, wholesalers, and/or contractors who are to furnish the transportation and/or other services specified. All vendors and suppliers are disclosed principals and independent contractors. As agent, the sole financial responsibility of the Agency is limited to the amount of commission it receives from said Suppliers in arranging said transportation or services on behalf of the named client.

This invoice is issued subject to any and all terms and conditions under which any transportation or other service is provided by the Suppliers. The Agency shall not become liable for any personal injury, property damage, accident, delay, inconvenience, change in itinerary or accommodations, or other irregularity which may occur due to (1) wrongful, negligent, or arbitrary acts or omissions on the part of the Suppliers, their employees, or others not in the direct control of the Agency; (2) defects or failures of any conveyance, equipment, or instrumentality under control of the Suppliers; and (3) and not limited to acts of God, acts of terrorism, fire, acts of governments or other authorities, wars, civil disturbances, riots, strikes, thefts, pilferage, epidemics, quarantines, or dangers incident to the sea, land, and air.

The client, by engaging the Agency and making deposit and/or full payment for the travel arrangements as specified, acknowledges the position of the Agency as stipulated by the foregoing; agrees to hold the Agency blameless in making the arrangements on his behalf, providing same shall be made through generally acceptable Suppliers at the time of engagement; and further agrees that restitution or damages, if any are claimed, shall be sought directly from the Suppliers. The client also agrees to the terms and conditions of the tour, cruise, or services as set forth in the brochures and/or circulars of the Suppliers.

Most cruise lines require the passenger to log on to their website prior to departure to fill out pre-cruise immigration and accept the terms and conditions of the passage contract. Should Kensington Cruises be asked to access the passenger booking prior to the client's log on, and be required to accept the passage contract on behalf of the client, Kensington Cruises and Montrose Travel shall not be liable for accepting the contract on behalf of the client. By signing the reservation authorization, client gives Kensington Cruises permission to accept the passage contract on their behalf and absolves Agency from any liability resulting in acceptance of the passage contract. Client is responsible for signing onto the supplier's website and reading the passage of contract themselves if Agency has accepted the contract on their behalf. Should client wish to have a copy of the passage of contract in writing, they may obtain one by requesting it from the Agency or the Supplier, or printing it themselves from Supplier's website. Agency is not responsible for providing the Supplier's passage of contract to the client unless it is specifically requested.

IMPORTANT INFORMATION

In the event of Kensington Cruises and/or Montrose Travel's default, you may be eligible for a refund of up to $15,000 from the California Travel Consumer Restitution Fund. If you were located in California at the time of your purchase, you have a right to make a claim against the Fund for a refund of any money paid to Montrose Travel that is due because of Montrose Travel's bankruptcy, insolvency, cessation of operations, or material failure to provide the transportation of travel services sold. The claim must be filed within 60 days (or in some limited circumstances, within one year) after you become aware of your loss. For a claim form and additional information, write to:

Travel Consumer Restitution Corporation
P. O. Box 8474
Northridge, CA 91327

DOCUMENTS – Please check your travel documents when you receive them. Be sure to proof your itinerary with your travel counselor. For cruises traveling to ports of call **including North America and in the Caribbean: All passengers must present a valid passport** and additionally consult their consulate (for their country of citizenship; i.e., the U.S. Consulate for U.S. citizens) concerning additional travel documentation or travel requirements for the countries being visited. If uncertain of travel requirements, use of a VISA service is recommended. Voter's registration, driver's licenses (except in closed loop cruises) and Social Security cards are not valid proof of citizenship. Resident aliens require a Resident Alien (Green) Card. Citizens of all other countries are required to provide a valid passport with a multiple U.S. re-entry visa, and should additionally consult their consulate of citizenship for additional travel documentation or requirements for the countries being visited. Please see www.travel.state.gov to confirm the appropriate Proof of Citizenship and/or inoculations required for your specific trip. Failure to provide appropriate, valid documentation may result in denied boarding for air, sea, and land conveyances, as well as out-of-pocket expenses. Kensington Cruises is not responsible if you do not have a valid passport or appropriate visas for your trip; this is the responsibility of the traveler.

BAGGAGE – Industry regulations require passenger's name on all checked baggage. Identification tags are available at the airport and cruise ship terminal. Most airlines are charging baggage fees for checked baggage. These fees range from $25 to $50 per bag and are payable directly to the airline. The fees for exceeding weight/size/quantity allowance on checked and/or carry-on luggage can be quite expensive. Contact your airline(s) for current information.

CHECK-IN – Allow a minimum check-in time of 2 hours for domestic and 3 hours for international flights. Times shown on your itinerary are from current schedules and are subject to change without notice.

RECONFIRMATION – Flight schedules change frequently and without notice. Reconfirm your first flight, continuing flights, and return flights. Reconfirm domestic flights 24 hours in advance and international flights 72 hours before departure. Reconfirmation is important to avoid inconveniences due to flight cancellations and to provide you with current flight schedules. Be sure to write down the name of the airline employee who confirms you.

TICKETS – Tickets that allow cancellation or use at a later date must be returned to Kensington Cruises for ticketing/tracking purposes. Cancelled or unused tickets must be returned for proper credit to your account. Lost, stolen, or destroyed tickets must be paid for until refund is received from the issuing carrier, subject to an airline-imposed service charge. In some situations the Supplier will not allow a refund.

CHANGE OF PLANS – If your plans change en route, you must contact the airline before the scheduled travel date and departure time. Some tickets issued on Promotional or Discounted fares may incur substantial penalties for changes or cancellation. Some tickets issued on Promotional or Discounted fares may lose their value if changes are made after the scheduled travel date for any segment. Some tickets issued on Promotional or Discounted fares are non-changeable.

INSURANCE – We strongly recommend the purchase of trip insurance to cover you in case of

- Default or bankruptcy of Suppliers
- Trip cancellation or interruption penalties (due to illness of yourself, travel companions, or family members)
- Baggage or personal possessions lost
- Emergency illness en route

Insurance cannot be purchased through the cruise line any later than the time of final payment for the specified cruise. Please read the cruise line brochure or check their website for complete details on the protection plan, including plan coverage, conditions, restrictions, limitations, and exclusions. Alternatively, you may purchase a policy through an independent travel insurance company – please ask Lori for details. After careful consideration, you may accept or decline the offered coverage. Please note that cruise line protection plans normally do not cover for pre-existing conditions – a passenger-protection plan that includes coverage for pre-existing conditions must be purchased within 15 to 20 days of deposit, and is available to you by calling Kensington Cruises.

CANCELLATIONS – Cancellations must be made in writing and sent with proof of delivery requiring signature to Kensington Cruises, 3010 Doyne Road, Pasadena, CA 91107. Cancellations **must be received prior to penalty date**. Cancellation by phone will not be accepted. Cancellation penalties apply as set by the individual cruise lines and may include contract, promotional, non-refundable, group, and cancelled airfare penalties. Penalties will begin on the penalty date listed on the front of this invoice. Be advised that Kensington Cruises has forwarded your payment for your cruise to the cruise line. Upon cancellation of your cruise, your refund (less any applicable penalties) will be returned to you by Kensington Cruises/MTravel only when we have received a refund from the Supplier. This refund can take up to eight (8) weeks from the cancellation date. On group bookings, the refund may be issued up to sixty (60) days after the sailing date. Unused airline tickets must be returned to Kensington Cruises with proof of delivery requiring signature. Please note that Kensington Cruises/MTravel assesses a non-refundable $50 cancellation fee once deposit has been made. This may or may not be covered by travel insurance.

ITINERARIES – It is the responsibility of the traveler to reconfirm his/her cruise itinerary with Kensington Cruises at least twelve (12) weeks prior to the sailing date. Kensington Cruises is not responsible for itinerary changes made subsequent to booking your cruise. When a client has not been given a cabin assignment and has booked on a "to be assigned" basis, it is understood and agreed that Kensington Cruises can make no guarantee on exact cabin accommodations or location. Cabin accommodations and assignments under these conditions are at the sole discretion of the cruise line. Without prior notice, Kensington Cruises reserves the right to upgrade passenger cabin assignments to higher cabin categories at no additional charge.

SPECIAL NEEDS – Passengers traveling who may require special needs, attention, or treatment must submit all special requirements in writing to Kensington Cruises at the time of booking. Special requirements and restrictions will apply to pregnant women, so please contact your cruise specialist. It is the traveler's responsibility to verify that Kensington Cruises has received the written request for special needs and/or requirements. Cruise lines reserve the right to refuse or revoke passage to anyone who is, in its sole judgment, in such physical or mental condition as to be unfit for travel or who may require care and attention beyond that which the ship can provide. Disabled passengers must be self-sufficient or travel with a passenger who will be responsible for any assistance needed during the cruise and in the event of emergency. Passengers confined to wheelchairs are advised that cabin doors are typically 22" wide, bathroom doors are 20" wide, and there is a 3" lip to the shower. Elevator service may or may not be available to all decks of the ship. Access to all public areas of ships is not guaranteed. Kensington Cruises is not responsible for any representations and/or omissions from the supplier that do not meet ADA regulations. Please note that on a cruise, not all ports are accessible, especially those that are reached via tenders. Passenger safety is the utmost concern of the ship, so it is up to the Captain to determine whether it is safe for a passenger confined to a wheelchair to be able to disembark via tender or a steep gangway. Kensington Cruises is not responsible for any ports missed due to the inability of the passenger to disembark if it is deemed unsafe by the ship's company.

Please consult with Lori as to your specific needs and specific information concerning your ship of choice.

NOTICE TO PASSENGERS TRAVELING BY AIR CARRIER – When air/common carrier is booked through the cruise line, the cruise line reserves the right to choose air carrier, routing, and gateway city airport terminal. Peak air travel dates and Alaska sailings may include non-prime air schedules, charters, and forced overnight hotel stays. Airline tickets issued by the cruise lines are highly restrictive. Fares used are based on "capacity controlled" criteria as well as contract, promotional, non-refundable, or group fares. Therefore, you may find that your air carrier ticket cannot be reissued, revalidated, or exchanged for another carrier or routing. Penalties may be imposed by the cruise line for airfare that is removed within 91 days of cruise departure. Schedules cannot be changed once your tickets have been issued. Travelers booked in the same cabin or traveling with other passengers are not guaranteed to receive routing on the same flight or carrier schedules. It is the sole responsibility of the traveler to reconfirm his/her round-trip flight times forty-eight (48) hours prior to departure with the assigned carrier. Kensington Cruises accepts no responsibility for flight schedule changes, missed connections, or problems that may result in the traveler missing their cruise.

AIR DEVIATION – At the written request of the traveler at 210 to 90 days in advance of sailing, Kensington Cruises will request deviation of air carrier transportation provided by the cruise line. A $50 to $75 per person deviation charge shall be imposed for each air deviation over and above any additional increase in airfare that may be imposed for said deviation. Deviation options and schedules are at the sole discretion of the cruise lines air/sea department. Any requested deviation shall be at the sole risk of the traveler and traveler is also advised that when there is a deviation from the cruise line transportation, all transfers provided by the cruise line become null and void.

PAYMENTS – Most cruise lines accept major credit cards, therefore Kensington Cruises will accept credit card payments and forward them to the cruise line. Checks must be made payable to Montrose Travel and be in U.S. funds drawn on a U.S. bank. Check payments made within 90 days of the sailing date must be made with a Certified Bank Check or Money Order. Cruise lines reserve the right to cancel any cruise not paid in full by its final payment due date without advance warning or notice; for this reason it is extremely important that all payments are received in advance of the cruise final payment due date. This invoice may not be used as a proof of payment, and all payments reflected on this invoice are subject to proof of payment such as credit card statements, cancelled check, or cash receipt. Without proof of payment, this invoice becomes null and void.

TAXES/SURCHARGES – Government taxes or Cruise Line Operational surcharges may be levied or changed at any time. If new taxes or surcharges are imposed or existing taxes or surcharges are increased after initial date of deposit, traveler will be responsible for payment of such taxes or surcharges.

PAST DUE ACCOUNTS – Purchaser agrees to pay Kensington Cruises all amounts due and owing FORTHWITH. In the event the amount due is not paid as agreed, a late payment service charge is imposed of 1½% per month of the amount due (18% annually). If suit is instituted to collect, Purchaser agrees to pay reasonable attorney's fees and costs. Acceptance of tickets and/or documents constitutes purchaser's agreement to the above conditions.

Reservation Authorization

After you review your Invoice and agree that all is correct, please complete, sign and return this Reservation Authorization immediately!

**** IMPORTANT INFORMATION ****

- **Your Travel Agent is:**____
- **Passenger Names:**____
- **Ship and Sailing date ~ Type of Cruise:**_____________________________
- **Booking #:**_____________________________
- Each traveler name must correspond exactly to the name on his/her valid government issued Photo I.D. used at check-In! Penalties will be assessed for name **CORRECTIONS!**
- Rates and fares are not guaranteed until your trip is paid in full

**** OPTIONAL INSURANCE ADVISORY ****

I ________ ACCEPT / ________ DECLINE Insurance from the cruise line: **Initials:** ____________

I ________ ACCEPT / ________ DECLINE Insurance from ________ Insurance company: **Initials:** ______

**** PAYMENT AUTHORIZATION ****

I hereby authorize 'Agency Name'* or its suppliers to charge the amounts listed on the attached "Invoice" to the following credit or debit card:

Print Exact Cardholder Name:			
CC Number:			
Credit Card Type:		Exp Date:	Security Code:
CC Billing Street Address:			
CC Billing City State Zip:			
CC Billing Phone:		Use same CC for all payments?	
Signature of Cardholder:			

By your signature below, you agree:

- that all traveler names correspond to the valid government photo I.D. that will be used at check-in.
- that the travel plans defined on your Invoice are correct as you requested.
- that you have read and agree to the "Limiting Terms and Conditions".
- that you will review your Invoice and, again, sign this authorization if it is sent to you to document changes to your original invoice.
- *your final documents cannot be released until this form is signed and returned.*

Your Signature: ***Date:***

* I understand that 'Agency Name' is affiliated as an independent contractor with 'Host Agency'

COMMISSION REPORT

Cruise Line/ Tour Co	Pax Name	Sailing or departure Date	Comm amount	Rcvd	Actual Amount

CRUISE RESERVATION FORM

Names_______________ DOB_______
_______________ DOB_______
_______________ DOB_______
_______________ DOB_______
Address_______________
City_______ St_______ ZIP_______
Ph(h)_______ Cel_______
Air City_______ C/O Y or N
Source of booking_______
Email _______

Dining: Early Late PC Confirmed W/L
Table Size 2 4 6 8
Seating with_______
Special Diet_______
Special Occasion_______

FARE		**TOTALS**	**C/L GROSS**
Fare	______x___	=______	______
Disc	______x___	=______	______
Sell	______x___	=______	______
3/4	______x___	=______	______
Air	______x___	=______	______
Land	______x___	=______	______
Insur	______x___	=______	______
AL HT	______x___	=______	______
Fuel	______x___	=______	______
Port	______x___	=______	______
Govt	______x___	=______	______
Trf	______x___	=______	______
Other	______x___	=______	______
TOT	______X___	=______	______
COM			______

Travel Ins. _______ Coverage pp_______
Purchased:_______ Y or N

Sailing Date_______ **Res#**_______
Res Agent_______ **Voy/Grp#**_______
Date Booked_______

Dep In House	______	$______
Dep remitted	______	To______
Mtravel comp	______	
Dep pkt sent	______	
Adv returned	______	
F/P reminder	______	
FP remitted	______	To______
Mtravel comp	______	
Docs in	______	
Docs checked	______	
Bon Voy gift	______	To______
Gift______	______	$______
Docs sent	______	
Welcome home	______	
Res cxld	______	To______

Cruise Line_______ Ship_______
Destination_______ #Nts_______
Cat_______ Gtee_______ Cbn#_______
Inside Outside Balc Suite
____

Air Dept Date_______ Rtn _______
Ports from/to_______

PAYMENT INFORMATION

Deposit pp_______x_______=_______
Option date_______ extend_______
Balance due $_______

Final Pymt date KC_______ C/L_______
Dep
CC#_______ **Exp**_______
Name_______ code_______
FP_______ Exp_______
Name_______ code_______
AMX Platinum tracking:_______ to:

Acknowledgements

A very special thanks to Kim Johnson of Cruise Navigators for teaching me how to be a cruise-selling travel agent, as well as for his creation of the first cruise reservation forms. Kim, you are a prince among many!

I'd also like to thank my dear friend, Jan Tuck, who has shown me that I can do anything if I just put my mind to it!

Lastly, special thanks to Andi McClure-Mysza and MTravel for their support these past few years, and also for their Limiting Terms and Conditions, and the basis of the Reservation Authorization form. If you are looking for a wonderful host agency, Andi is the person to contact! MTravel has been a fantastic home for Kensington Cruises for the past few years!

Dayle Dermatis, you are the shining star who brought the whole thing together for me! Thank you for your wealth of experience and knowledge of the independent publishing world. Your copy-editing and formatting of the book was invaluable – I couldn't have done it without you!

A special shout out to Stojan Mihajlov for his beautiful book cover! I found Stojan through www.99designs.com, where you can have artists from all over the world compete to design your book cover. Stojan, you gave the book its identity, and you did a gorgeous job! Thank you!

About the Author

Lori has been selling cruises since 1984. She started in reservations at Princess Cruises and worked her way up to eventually working as liaison between the ships and the home office. In 1988 she went to work onboard the original *Love Boat* for the Mediterranean and Baltic Season and got to climb the pyramids, walk in the steps of Jesus, navigate past the Arctic Circle, and meet some of the most extraordinary people. After returning home, she began selling cruises as a travel agent and never looked back. She has been featured in numerous magazines, is a Master Cruise Counselor through CLIA, and is considered an expert in her field.

She now lives in California with her two children and tries to take at least two cruises a year. She has met some of her dearest friends onboard ships and considers herself very fortunate indeed to have been able to cruise the world. She hopes this book opens doors for you so that you, too, can experience the world from the balcony of your very own stateroom!

Made in the USA
Columbia, SC
10 November 2024

46096685R00095